Tustin

as It Once Was

TUSTIN

AS IT ONCE WAS

Juanita Lovret

THE History PRESS

Published by The History Press
Charleston, SC 29403
www.historypress.net

Front cover image: The author's grandparents, E.S. and Maud Jones, built this house in the late 1800s in the middle of their newly planted orange orchard. *Courtesy of the author.*
Back cover image: Tustin Packing Company opened in 1905 in an old warehouse on Newport Avenue. It employed fifty workers. *Courtesy of Tustin Area Museum.*

First published 2011
Manufactured in the United States
ISBN 978.1.60949.461.2

Library of Congress Cataloging-in-Publication Data

Lovret, Juanita.
Tustin as it once was / Juanita Lovret.
p. cm.
A collection of articles from the Tustin news column "Remember when."
ISBN 978-1-60949-461-2
1. Tustin (Calif.)--History. 2. Tustin (Calif.)--Social life and customs. I. Tustin news. II. Title.
F869.T88L68 2011
979.4'96--dc23
2011038705

Notice: The information in this book is true and complete to the best of our knowledge. It is offered without guarantee on the part of the author or The History Press. The author and The History Press disclaim all liability in connection with the use of this book.

Contents

Acknowledgments

Jill Leach, editor of the *Tustin News* at the time, spurred my interest in history in 1997 when she convinced me to write a column entitled "Remember When," based on my memories of Tustin. Without her persuasion, plus the encouragement and aid of many others, the five-hundred-plus columns that inspired this book would never have materialized.

First Marsha Lundin and now Barbara Hannigan and Bill Finken in the Tustin Area Museum office have offered ideas and interrupted their work to help me with research as well as to find photos. Compliments and praise from the readers of the *Tustin News* have maintained my interest. These people, plus many others—such as my husband, Clint, who proofreads my work, and Guy Ball, a computer genius who has shared his knowledge and skills, as well as encouragement when I have become frustrated—have earned my deepest gratitude and thanks.

I couldn't have done it without you!

Introduction

Memories of Old Tustin

As we look at the intersection of Main and D (El Camino Real) today, it is difficult to realize that these four corners were the heart of Tustin's commercial district for almost one hundred years until the mid 1950s, when housing tracts began to replace orange orchards and shopping centers were built to serve the hundreds of new residents.

When Tustin was being settled, Fourth Street, as it was labeled on Columbus Tustin's plat map, soon became known as Main Street because it was the principal street in the tiny village, with L. Utt Pioneer Store, Dr. Levi Fuller's drugstore, the post office, the Tustin Building, a blacksmith and later the Bank of Tustin all located here. The name stuck, and Fourth Street was soon forgotten.

When I was a kid, a trip to Tustin from our orange ranch outside town began with a stop at the First National Bank of Tustin, successor to the Bank of Tustin, on the corner of Main and D (El Camino Real). After her transaction was completed, my mother would linger to chat with Frances Logan, the longtime teller who knew everything that happened in Tustin. While they were gossiping, I would admire the ornate Victorian woodwork and fancy iron work on the teller windows. Teller Bill Leinberger would probably be talking with someone. Mr. Vance—Charlie to those who knew him well—the cashier, would probably be occupied at his desk, perhaps making a loan to a farmer who was waiting for the packinghouse to send him a check for his orange crop.

As we left the bank, I'd wonder how many feet had passed over the worn concrete stoop since it had been installed in 1888. Practically everyone in town banked here. Grammar school children learned about thrift by hoarding their pennies and walking to the bank as a class each month to deposit them.

Mother and I usually had many other errands. First, we'd visit Mrs. Gowdy at the Tustin Library and check out a few books. Then we'd cross to the drugstore to pick up toothpaste or other items. If it was a hot day, we'd climb up on the stools at the counter and have a Coke or soda.

Buying stamps at the post office down the street or picking up clothes at the cleaners or leaving my dad's watch at the jewelry shop for repair might be next on our to-do list. Usually we'd stop at Cox's Market or Carter's grocery store. Both had meat counters with butchers who gave Mother the best cuts of meat, but I was more interested in the big box with the round lids that housed the ice cream. Ice cream was a special treat since we only had an ice box at home.

Big John Stanton might be pulling up alongside the drugstore in his police vehicle as we returned to our car. He always nodded politely to Mother and me. I was a little afraid of him since I'd been frightened by the siren on his police car when he once took off after a speeder while we waited on the corner to cross D Street.

Mother would have liked to browse at Crawford's Frock Shop, which was located nearby in the little building that had been the office of Dr. Sheldon, Tustin's first doctor, and check out Tustin Hardware's merchandise, as well as the new plants at Piepers Feed Store, but there was no time, as it was almost noon. Dad would be coming in from tractoring and expect his dinner.

The Tustin Billiard Hall was the only place we never visited in downtown Tustin, now called Old Town. Mother didn't even like to walk past it and always cautioned me to look the other way.

Many of the stories in this book were sparked by my childhood memories of Tustin as a small vibrant commercial center, plus stories told by my mother, my aunts and uncle of their childhoods in the very early days of the village founded by Columbus Tustin. Our family has been part of the area since 1885, when my grandparents bought barren land and turned it into a ranch outside of the tiny, fledgling settlement. Mother, her sisters and brother grew up with the town. I've spent my life in the wonderful community that resulted. Now my grandchildren are the ones listening to tales of the small town Tustin once was, as they enjoy the metropolitan area it has become.

Chapter 1

Tustin's Early Years

Jose Antonio Yorba Sells Rancho to Developers

Looking down on what could be a Monopoly board of houses and buildings as you fly over the Tustin area, en route to John Wayne airport, it is easy to forget that the area was covered with wild mustard, oak and sycamore trees when the first inhabitants, the California Indians, lived there.

Hunters and gatherers, they lived off the land and migrated from location to location to find game and food. The only buildings were small thatched huts called wickiups.

Spanish explorers visited the California coast beginning in 1500, but not until 1769 did the first white men—Spanish missionaries Father Juan Crespi and Father Francisco Gomez, traveling with Don Gaspar de Portola, governor of Lower California, and a company of four officers and sixty-three men—entered the area that is now Orange County. They camped briefly, but no white men settled here until 1776, when Mission San Juan Capistrano was founded.

Spanish soldiers arriving with the missionaries established homes, spreading out as far as what is now Olive. They eventually petitioned the Spanish government for the properties, and the Rancho Period began. Rancho Santiago de Santa Ana, which would eventually become Tustin, Santa Ana, Orange, Olive, El Modena, Costa Mesa and part of Newport, was granted to Jose Antonio Yorba by the king of Spain in 1809. After

Mexico won its freedom from Spain in 1821 and control of Alta California, land grants became more numerous.

Years passed, many of the original grantees died and the ranchos were divided among their heirs. They lived luxuriously and were unprepared for a disastrous two-year drought. Needing funds, they sold their ranchos to opportunists who later transferred their shares to men like Columbus Tustin who established small communities. Outlying areas were subdivided into small farms and orchards.

Thousands of acres went to big investors, including James Irvine, who acquired Rancho San Joaquin, Rancho Lomas de Santiago and a strip of Rancho Santiago de Santa Ana to form the Irvine Ranch. The ranch remained one of the largest landholders in Orange County for many years despite selling off land over time. No longer farming, the company is now developing forty-four thousand acres of master-planned communities, in addition to setting aside fifty thousand acres for wilderness and recreational preserves.

A very early Irvine sale was a 1,700-acre parcel, part of the Rancho Santiago de Santa Ana acquisition, bought in 1910 by George E. Marcy, a Chicago meatpacker. Marcy built ranch headquarters on Newport Avenue near the present Marcy Drive and hired Albert A. Leake as ranch superintendent. Although the Marcys visited from Chicago at intervals, Leake was responsible for the property, which included citrus orchards and grazing land as well as a park with a lake, swans and peacocks.

George E. Marcy, a wealthy Chicago meatpacker, was one of those who bought large parcels of wild, untamed land. He purchased 1,700 acres of wilderness east of Tustin in 1910 and turned it into citrus orchards and grazing land, as well as a park. The land was subdivided as Cowan Heights and Peacock Hill in the 1950s. *Courtesy of Tustin Area Museum.*

The peaceful, agrarian atmosphere of the area was shattered after World War II, as a blight infected the citrus orchards and former servicemen demanded housing. Walter H. Cowan, a retired oil executive, purchased 822 acres of barren land from Marcy in 1944 and began developing Cowan Heights as a residential area. Later Don Shanahan, a Southern California builder, bought the Marcy Ranch headquarters and surrounding citrus orchards to develop as Peacock Hill. Soon the remainder of the ranch was being developed as a residential area.

Unable to resist the dollars offered by developers, others joined the trend to sell, resulting in today's widespread development.

Columbus Tustin Launches City of Dreams

As January 1, 1870, approached, Columbus Tustin was making plans for his share of the undivided Rancho Santiago de Santa Ana property he and Nelson Stafford had purchased for $5,000 in the summer of 1863.

Columbus Tustin bought the nucleus of today's Tustin, a scant one thousand acres of Rancho Santiago de Santa Ana, in 1868 for $2,900 and began to lay out the city of his dreams. The way was long and hard, and he died before he saw his plans come to fruition, but eventually the tide turned, and Tustin was on its way to being the successful city it is today. *Courtesy of Tustin Area Museum.*

After the court approved partitioning the rancho, he and Stafford took title to a specific parcel of land, which they promptly divided in half. Tustin acquired just over 839 acres from the original purchase and bought an additional 159 acres from Stafford for $400. His total cost for just under 1,000 acres was $2,900.

The property, destined to become the nucleus of today's Tustin, extended from the present-day Lyon Street to Newport Avenue. Sycamore, elderberry and alder trees, wild yellow mustard, wild flowers and prickly pear cactus and cholla covered it. The only inhabitants were deer, squirrels, badgers, rabbits, owls, doves and small game.

Most people think Columbus Tustin gave his name to the town, but Mrs. Montgomery G. Rice, granddaughter of Charles Wilcox, an early Tustin resident, disputed this. She claimed that Stella Preble Nau, daughter of another Tustin pioneer, always said the name Tustin was given to the community because, in the beginning, people referred to it as Tustin's land or would say "See Tustin to buy property," and gradually, the place became known by that name.

Tustin is thought to have filed the original plat map for Tustin City in 1870 or 1871, but there is no firm record of it. There is a record, however, of his sister, Barbara, being the first person to purchase land from him. She bought for $2,400 117 acres in August 1870. She later sold it back to him and bought and subdivided 50 acres near B Street. In an 1871 purchase, she acquired 50 acres near McFadden. Others gradually purchased property. Most were speculators who bought large blocks of land but did not establish homes or businesses to strengthen the fledgling community.

But by 1874 people were beginning to take root in Tustin. Writing in *The History of Orange County*, published by Mrs. J.E. Pleasants in 1931, C.E. Utt recalled that when his family arrived in June 1874, there was a school and the Sycamore School District had been established, with about a dozen families living within its boundaries.

Tustin began giving a lot to anyone who would build on it, and soon there were three stores, a meat market, a tin shop, a saloon and a gristmill. This prosperity ended in 1877 when the Southern Pacific Railway extended its line from Anaheim. Santa Ana, not Tustin, won the competition for the terminus. Businesses left and Tustin became, in Utt's words, a "dead city."

The post office and Utt's Pioneer Store continued to serve the residents. Tustin gradually began to rebuild, bolstered by the boom of the 1880s. New businesses opened, including the Bank of Tustin in 1887. The First Advent Christian Church organized in 1880; Tustin Presbyterian Church opened its first sanctuary in 1884.

The tide had turned, and Tustin was on its way to becoming the successful city it is today.

City Plat Map Sets Aside Block for Schools

In planning Tustin City, Columbus Tustin provided well for the children who would live there. The plat map he created for his development set aside an entire block between Second and Third Streets and B and C Streets as the School Block. Two years later, on February 5, 1872, the Los Angeles County Board of Supervisors—Orange County had not yet been formed—created the Sycamore School District.

Miss Anna Casad (or Cozad)—records disagree on spelling—was hired to teach for sixty dollars per month. A house on the southwest corner of the

This building housed Tustin's only school from 1890 to 1914, when it was replaced by a grammar school and a primary school. The bell that hung in the belfry now stands in front of the Tustin Unified School District administration building, which occupies a site on C Street very close to where this school was located. *Courtesy of Tustin Area Museum.*

School Block became Tustin's first school, opening on February 12, 1872, with about twenty-eight students.

A two-story building with two rooms on each floor replaced this school in 1882. Orange County was formed in 1889, and the school district became Tustin School District.

Principal John J. Zielian grew tired of coping with the inconvenience of the old four-room schoolhouse, which he described as a "nightmare." At his urging, a four-room addition costing $7,000 was added in 1890. Students came from El Modena, Costa Mesa and El Toro, as well as Tustin. He added a ninth grade for students wanting to continue their education. The few wishing even more education went to Santa Ana High School, which opened in 1889.

Many students, including my mother and her siblings, came to school on horseback or in a horse-drawn buggy. The animals were housed in the stable next to the playground, which was divided to separate the boys from the girls.

By the time I was ready for school, the old school was gone, replaced by two buildings in 1914. The primary school of kindergarten, first, second and third grades faced Main Street next to the Presbyterian Church. A two-story grammar school housed fourth through eighth grades on the north end of the School Block, facing C Street. Playing fields extended to First Street. After graduation, I attended Tustin Union High School, which had opened in 1922 on Laguna Road.

The current neighborhood school concept replaced the primary and elementary schools in the 1960s, and the old buildings were razed. Foothill High opened in 1963 to ease the crowding at Tustin. The original Tustin High was rebuilt to meet earthquake standards in 1966. Beckman opened in 2004 to accommodate housing developments east of Tustin.

The School Block no longer has any schools on it. Tustin Unified School District offices, the Senior Center and Pepper Tree Park currently occupy the land.

SETTLERS DISCOVER TUSTIN

Tustin City was mainly a concept in Columbus Tustin's head 150 years ago, yet settlers—such as Lysander Utt, his wife, Emily Arvilla Pratt, and his young son, Charles Edward "C.E."—came long distances to make their home here.

Although Tustin had prepared a plat map several years earlier, the development he visualized had not yet materialized when they arrived in Tustin City by covered wagon on June 5, 1874. C.E., who was eight at that time, wrote years later that "Tustin City consisted of a big sounding name, a small store and a blacksmith shop with a few settlers' shacks hidden around in the thickets of wild mustard."

A native of Virginia, Utt had traveled to California early in the gold rush years. He met and married his wife in the gold country, and they established a home in Placer County where C.E., their only child, was born. Samuel Armor, writing in *History of Orange County*, described Utt as a man who traveled the Santa Fe Trail a number of times before the Mexican War of 1846–1848 and made and lost several fortunes.

The family made the month-long trip south in a covered wagon. On the last night, they camped on the banks of the Coyote Creek near the present community of Buena Park, elated because they were almost at their destination. Traveling eastward through Anaheim, Orange (called Richland at that time) and Santa Ana, they would reach Tustin City. Unfortunately, as C.E. often explained, they missed Tustin City and didn't realize it until they arrived at the San Joaquin Ranch and the cabin of Arvilla's brother, Charlie Platt.

Tustin City had no available housing, but the second floor of the general store that dominated the center of town was empty. Built to be a hotel, the structure had been reclaimed by Langenberger and Brockman lumber dealers when the owner couldn't pay for the construction materials and sold to H.H. Dickerman, who operated the general store.

The Utt family moved into these quarters, and Mrs. Utt began to take in boarders. When Dickerman died a short time later, Utt bought the building and changed the sign in front to read "L. Utt Pioneer Store." C.E. attended Tustin Grammar School, helped in the store and hired out to do farm work.

After Utt died sixteen years later, C.E. ran the store for a year before taking a partner, Perry Lewis. In 1893, they sold it to A. Getty and Company, and C.E. started his successful career as a farmer, businessman and civic leader. Over the years, he raised almost every crop grown in the area, from citrus to peanuts and chili peppers. He organized the San Joaquin Fruit Company; served as president of the First National Bank of Tustin; rescued the Willard Water Works from bankruptcy, renaming it Tustin Water Works; and started the Utt Grape Juice Company to use his surplus grapes.

L. Utt Pioneer Store, one of the earliest businesses in Tustin City, anchored the commercial section of Main Street. The Utt family came to Tustin in 1874 and lived in rooms over the general store in a building that had originally been intended for a hotel. Mrs. Utt put the space to use by taking in boarders. *Courtesy of Tustin Area Museum.*

He married Mary Sheldon, daughter of another pioneer family, and they had five children before her death in 1918, one of whom, James B., became a U.S. congressman. Utt later married widow Margaret Rawlings.

The family is commemorated in Tustin by C.E. Utt Middle School and Utt Drive.

SANTA ANA AND TUSTIN FIGHT FOR RAILROAD

Tustin and Santa Ana have fought over many things, but one of the biggest battles was the fight for the Southern Pacific Railroad back in the 1800s.

Southern Pacific had extended its tracks from Los Angeles to Anaheim by 1874 and wanted to keep going with a station in either Tustin or Santa Ana. Both towns vied for the prize, but according to Stephen Donaldson, a railroad historian, Santa Ana won by offering $10,000 in cash, land for a depot and a free right of way through town.

The station was completed, and Southern Pacific arrived in 1877 in Santa Ana, a village of about five hundred people. Despite having lost the prestige of the station, the people of Tustin had achieved a way to reach Los Angeles without spending a day traveling by horse-drawn wagon or buggy.

But the privilege cost them dearly. Taking advantage of their monopoly, Southern Pacific charged four dollars—a tremendous sum at that time—for the three-hour trip to Los Angeles. Freight rates were equally high for farmers and merchants who complained that Southern Pacific was gouging the public and putting a stranglehold on the local economy.

This monopoly was broken when the Atchison, Topeka and Santa Fe in 1887 extended its line from Riverside to Santa Ana, threatening to cut into SP's trade. Southern Pacific responded by extending the line from Anaheim south into Tustin along Esplanade and building a large, two-story depot with freight facilities on Newport Avenue, south of Main Street. The train made two trips a day into Los Angeles, overnighting at the Tustin station where it was reversed on a turn table.

Collis Huntington, president of Southern Pacific, considered one of the most powerful economic forces in California, was still fuming over James Irvine Sr.'s refusal to let Southern Pacific lay tracks across the Irvine Ranch back in 1877. With a base in Tustin, he was determined that his railroad would make use of this most direct route between Los Angeles and San Diego.

Tustin, which lost the fight with Santa Ana for the Southern Pacific Railroad depot back in1877, finally got its own station when Southern Pacific extended its line south from Anaheim into Tustin about ten years later. The train, which carried passengers into Los Angeles and back twice a day in the beginning, eventually hauled oranges from the local packinghouses. *Courtesy of Tustin Area Museum.*

One Sunday morning in 1888, a Southern Pacific crew began laying track from the Tustin terminus to the edge of the Irvine Ranch. They planned to lay as much track as possible while the courts were closed for the weekend, but they hadn't reckoned with Irvine ranch hands who faced the track crew with guns drawn and threatened to open fire if the workers attempted to cross the Irvine property.

The track layers backed off, and on Monday, Irvine Ranch officials obtained a court order, blocking Southern Pacific from the ranch. Irvine then gave Santa Fe the right to cross the ranch, and the track, which is still used today, was extended between Santa Ana and San Diego. The unused SP track south of Tustin was torn up in 1910.

Although passenger service to Tustin halted temporarily in 1903 and permanently in 1923, Southern Pacific continued to haul oranges from local packinghouses on the Tustin line until the bridge across the Santiago Creek washed out during heavy rain in the 1960s. The station was eventually torn down and the tracks removed. The walking path that runs along Esplanade in North Tustin uses the property once owned by the railroad.

Blacksmith Necessary in New Community

Records are skimpy, but photos and memoirs show that Samuel Eddy was an early Tustin blacksmith. His shop occupied the southwest corner of Third and B Streets in the late 1800s. A trustee of the Sycamore School District from 1882 to 1885, Eddy and his wife were active members of the First Advent Christian Church. It is possible that his son, Ralph, also a blacksmith, kept the business open after his father's death because Mrs. Eddy bought a house on the opposite corner and continued to live in the neighborhood.

Other early photos show another blacksmith shop, possibly on the north side of Main Street between C and D (El Camino Real), that was said to be owned by a man named Marlow. Later photos show that John Wing had a blacksmith shop in 1919 at the same location, assisted by a man named Darnell.

Tom Wilson, who came to Tustin about this time, opened a new blacksmith shop on C Street across from the Tustin Grammar School. With the combination of more modern equipment, skill and courtesy, he soon built a profitable and permanent business.

This blacksmith and shoeing shop owned by John Wing is thought to have been located at the corner of Main and C Streets, across from the First Presbyterian Church. A blacksmith shop was a very necessary establishment in the early days of Tustin. The shady spot was later used by the men in the Tustin Horseshoe Club. *Courtesy of Tustin Area Museum.*

A native of Idaho, Wilson had moved in 1897 to Omaha, Nebraska, and apprenticed himself to a horseshoer. After learning that trade, he took up general blacksmithing. During the Spanish-American War, he served in the navy as a blacksmith on the armored cruiser, *Brooklyn*, in the Battle of Santiago.

He later saw service in the Philippines and during the Boxer uprising in China. He was proud of having visited nearly every important port in the Orient.

When his enlistment expired, he returned to San Francisco to be discharged. He then worked in Moore, Montana, as a blacksmith before coming to Tustin.

Wilson and his wife, Mertie, had a daughter, Mertie Marie. The family belonged to the First Advent Christian Church. He was a member of both the Knights of Pythias and the Masonic Lodge.

Today, the building that housed Wilson's shop is owned by Victor Andersen, a blacksmith for over sixty years, and the business continues. One of the few remaining smithies in the Southland, he comes from his home in Orange each morning to open the doors at seven. Clients bring gates, lamps and even exercise equipment for him to mend using the traditional old tools plus modern welding equipment.

Blacksmithing once involved repairing farm equipment and shoeing horses, but horses today are shod by professionals who generally travel to their clients by truck. Now that Tustin's orange groves have been replaced by houses, there isn't much farm equipment left to repair, but the tin-roofed barn that houses Anderson's shop is still a jumble of items waiting to be repaired.

Civil War Vets Discover Tustin

Large numbers of Civil War veterans, both Union and Confederate, came to Southern California after the cessation of hostilities with General Lee's surrender to General Grant at Appomattox. Many, with and without families, chose to settle in the recently formed Tustin City.

Discussing this movement west, Lou Carlson, chaplain for the Orange County chapter of the Sons of Confederate Veterans, said that "the South was in ruins. The North had the postwar problem of a huge labor force arriving. Employment was a problem. In addition to the veterans returning home, large numbers of freed slaves moved to the North after the war."

Gordon Bricken, who plans to assemble a book with brief biographies of all Civil War veterans buried in Santa Ana Cemetery, added that "virtually all the leaders of the movement to secede from Los Angeles County and create Orange County in the 1880s were Confederate veterans."

Dr. William Burgess Wall, who was to contribute a great deal to Orange County, came to Tustin in 1875 after serving as a surgeon in the Confederate States of America's Mississippi Thirty-third Infantry. He planted what was considered to be Tustin's first citrus grove on forty acres south of Seventeenth on the east side of Tustin Avenue.

Peter T. Adams, another Southerner who had served as a lieutenant colonel in Company B of Colonel McCord's Texas Regiment, CSA, arrived in Tustin from Texas in 1877 and purchased land west of Williams and south of Main Street, near where Heideman School is today, which he planted with citrus. He and his wife, the former Henrietta Downs, had five children.

Charles F. Bennett, a lieutenant in Company G, Fifty-fifth Infantry, Grand Army of the Republic (GAR), fought in thirty-two engagements, including Shiloh and Vicksburg. After coming to Tustin in 1885, he bought twenty-two acres on the east side of Tustin Avenue near Wall's acreage to build a home and plant a citrus grove.

He also owned sixty acres of citrus in El Toro and became an authority on irrigation of oranges, often attending national irrigation conferences. He served in the California legislature as a Seventy-sixth District assemblyman from 1893 to 1895.

H.H. Higbey, a veteran of Company E, Fifteenth Iowa Infantry, GAR, also became an orchardist after coming to Tustin in 1897. He grew oranges, walnuts and apricots on twelve acres on Sixth Street. George Washington Hubbard, Company I, Sixteenth Infantry, New York, GAR, came to Tustin in 1883 and bought forty acres that he planted with oranges, apricots and walnuts.

The many Civil War veterans, both Union and Confederate, who helped settle early Tustin are remembered by the theme of this Knights of Pythias Lodge No. 85 parade float, the Blue and Gray. Although some turned to business, most of the Civil War veterans coming to Tustin purchased acreage and established successful orange groves. *Courtesy of Tustin Area Museum.*

Although many of the veterans coming to Tustin bought land and planted orchards, others elected to pursue different interests. H.W. Smith, a corporal in Company A, Thirteenth Regiment, Michigan, GAR, came to Tustin in 1901 and opened a real estate office with J.A. Phiney as his partner. Later in 1919, he served as Tustin Township justice of the peace.

W.G. Haskins, Company C, 51st Infantry, Massachusetts, GAR, was a trustee of the Tustin School District from 1896 to 1900. James H. Brown, who received a Medal of Honor for his service in the United States Navy, was an active member of the First Advent Christian Church.

These men and the vast majority of CSA and GAR veterans who came to Orange County are buried in Santa Ana Cemetery next to Fairhaven Memorial Park. They have been honored each Memorial Day since at least 1881 when Grand Army of the Republic veterans from the General John Sedgwick Post No. 17 held the first services.

Mail Arrives by Stage Coach

As with many events in Tustin's history, two versions exist regarding the first post office in the community. "Official" records indicate that the first post office was established August 10, 1880, in the Tustin Building on the south side of Main, east of C Street, with Columbus Tustin as postmaster; however, Perry E. Lewis, whose father, H.B. Lewis, came to Tustin in 1876, disputed this, remembering that Nathan T. Harris, known as a deputy postmaster, distributed mail from his house on the southwest corner of Second and B Streets prior to that time.

Everyone seems to agree that the mail was brought to Tustin by stage coach in the early days. People would gather in front of the post office when the stage arrived, and the postmaster would distribute the letters and parcels directly from the mail sack.

Columbus Tustin turned the job of postmaster over to his daughter, Martha, in 1883. She served until near the end of 1889, when H.B. Lewis replaced her. During these years, Tustin acquired new residents and the post office became a busy place, needing larger quarters. A small building was erected east of the Tustin Building to meet the need.

On days when the mail was expected, people would begin to collect in front of the post office and the Tustin Building on the south side of Main Street, anxiously awaiting the arrival of the stage coach. The postmaster would distribute letters and parcels directly from the mail sack without going into the tiny post office where patrons had boxes. *Courtesy of Tustin Area Museum.*

William Huntley, who came to Tustin in 1886, remembered:

> *The post office was small, not more than 12 or 16 feet square and surrounded on two sides by a larger room. This made it possible to do business at the window without blocking traffic on the sidewalk. It also allowed access to the lock boxes which were at your right as you stood at the window. There were few lock boxes, probably not more than 50. Later, as population increased, boxes were placed on the east wall. This arrangement made it possible to get at your post office box any time, as there was no door to this outer room.*

After the arrival of the railroad, Tustin sent and received mail from Aliso Station, south of town. Franklin P. Crawford transported the mail bags between the post office and the station. The outgoing mail bag was placed on a hook alongside the Santa Fe track and snagged by an arm extended from the passing train. The incoming mail bag was kicked out the baggage car door as the train went by. Eventually mail, both incoming and outgoing, passed through the Santa Ana post office.

The post office was relocated to the Knights of Pythias building on the north side of Main in 1925. In 1951, it was moved to the north side of West Third off C Street. Albert Downs followed Lewis as postmaster. Other postmasters and postmistresses over the years include Fannie Tustin, A.D. Turner, J.A. Phiney, Florence Stone, Mamie Phiney, Cinderella Phiney, Sam Long and Carolyn Campbell, who served the longest, from 1943 to 1955.

The present modern concrete block post office at 340 East First Street was dedicated with Jess J. Parks as postmaster and Ray S. Kingsbury as assistant postmaster in 1962, ending the days of the small post office where friends met to chat.

Chapter 2

Years of Growth and Change

Boom of 1880s Brings Prosperity and Society

By the boom of the 1880s, a time of prosperity in Southern California, Tustin had grown from a small frontier settlement of shacks to a lovely community with tree-lined streets and beautiful Victorian houses.

Wealthy people who were used to being socially active came to Tustin from cities such as San Francisco and Cincinnati. Before long they were hosting elegant parties. Evenings in their homes were devoted to programs of violin, piano and vocal selections. Poetry readings and dramatic skits were organized. Attendance at the Opera House in Santa Ana swelled. Culture and self-improvement became popular.

David Hewes, a wealthy San Francisco contractor, and his second wife, Matilda, came to Tustin in 1881, seeking a mild climate more suited to her health than the dampness of the Bay Area. Soon after their magnificent Victorian home was completed at the corner of Main and B Streets, Mrs. Hewes's daughter and son-in-law, Franklina and William S. Bartlett, also moved to Tustin. The two couples became active members of Tustin society.

Mrs. Bartlett missed the educational stimulation she had experienced in an Oakland organization based on the philosophy of Dr. Adrien Ebell, a Berlin, Germany scholar who visualized a world movement "to promote the development of the feminist mind in the systematic study of the exact science, including music, art and language."

No doubt the newly organized Ebell Club of the Santa Ana Valley was discussed when Miss Stella Preble, *left*, and Miss Jeannette Wilcox met for tea. Miss Wilcox later married Adolph A. Kraft in a fancy wedding, and Miss Preble became Mrs. S.W. Nau. Both women were popular in Tustin's social circles. *Courtesy of Tustin Area Museum.*

As the first president of the Ebell Society of Oakland, Mrs. Bartlett had helped organize a program of monthly meetings. After she moved to Southern California, she was asked to aid in organizing the Los Angeles Ebell Society. Then she decided Tustin needed such an organization.

It didn't take long for her to arouse the interest of a number of Tustin women, including Mrs. E.D. Buss, wife of the cashier of the Bank of Tustin and a member of the school board; Mrs. Edward M. Neally, whose husband was a citrus grower, secretary-treasurer of the Tustin Protective Association and a school board member, and Stella Preble, who became Mrs. S.W. Nau, socialite and wife of a citrus grower.

The Ebell Club of the Santa Ana Valley formed in 1894 with seventy charter members, including many from Tustin. Meetings were held at various locations in Santa Ana—the Rossmore Hotel, the Opera House and the Presbyterian Church—but by 1924, when there were hundreds of members, the ladies decided they needed their own clubhouse. Frederick Ely, a prominent Santa Ana architect, designed a 12,400-square-foot

Spanish Colonial clubhouse to be built in the French Park section of Santa Ana by Sam Preble, a Tustin contractor. The building has been listed on the National Register of Historic Places since 2001.

Fraternal Organizations Form

Tustin had three fraternal organizations back in the 1880s, the Independent Order of Odd Fellows, the I.O.G.F., and the Order of the Knights of Pythias. Only the K of P, which was chartered in 1882, still meets.

Affiliated with the Order of Knights of Pythias, an international, nonsectarian fraternal order founded in Washington, D.C., on February, 18, 1864, by Justice T. Rathbone and the first fraternal order to be chartered by an Act of Congress, the organization aimed to heal the wounds between the North and South, promote friendship among men and relieve suffering. Tustin Lodge No. 85 is one of more than two thousand in the United States and Canada.

Order of Knights of Pythias Lodge No. 85 was chartered in Tustin in 1882 and met for years on the second floor of the Bank of Tustin building, which became a drugstore when the bank closed, then the First National Bank. The lodge built its own building across the street in 1925 on property that had belonged to C.E. Utt. *Courtesy of Tustin Area Museum.*

The Tustin lodge met for many years in rooms on the second floor of the First National Bank of Tustin building. Then in 1925, they bought the property on the northeast corner of Main and D (El Camino Real) from C.E. Utt and had a two-story Neoclassical commercial building constructed. Their lodge hall and offices occupy the entire second floor, with the lower level available for shops, offices and businesses.

The Knight of Pythias building has housed many tenants, including Tustin's first city hall from 1927 to 1949 and the Tustin post office, 1930 to 1949. Tustin Variety Store and Tustin Drug Store were longtime occupants on the D Street side of the building. Tustin Shoe Shop and Tustin Radio Shop were tenants on the Main Street side. Present occupants include the Tustin Area Museum.

As an adjunct to the lodge, Pythian Sisters, Tustin Temple No. 27, was chartered in 1923. About fifty wives of members joined this group. Knights of Pythias members and the women of its auxiliary were counted among the social leaders of Tustin. A wit once said, "To be somebody in Tustin, you have to belong to the Knights of Pythias, American Legion and Tustin Presbyterian Church."

In addition to doing charitable work, the group sponsored dances and socials for members and guests. Pythian Sisters were excellent cooks and published a cookbook that became a best-seller. As the lodge members aged, the membership dwindled and the Pythian Sisters disbanded; however, lodge membership has risen in recent years.

The building, which the lodge still owns, is considered a candidate for the National Register on the basis of its architecture, quality construction, high degree of original integrity and significance in Tustin history, according to a City of Tustin Historical Survey by Thirtieth Street Architects, Inc. Most of the characteristics of its 1920s architecture remain, including matching bay windows on the lower floor with the enclosed main entrance to the second level centered between them. Also in keeping with the architecture of this period is the section of glass brick embedded in the floor at the entrance to the Tustin Area Museum to allow natural light to filter into the basement.

Look up the next time you pass the gold and brown textured brick structure, and you will see the colorful Knights of Pythias emblem that confirms its early chartering and identifies it as Lodge No. 85.

Adventists Organize First Church

Tustin had no churches for the first ten years of its existence. Settlers tended to gather according to denomination in the hall above Columbus Tustin's store or the school house for prayer meetings.

"The Adventists were the most numerous of those early Christian denominations settled in Tustin," according to Ray Elmer Dawson in *A History of Tustin California*, which was first written as his thesis for a master of arts degree at the University of Southern California in 1938 while he was a teacher at Tustin Grammar School.

They also were the first to organize. Carolyn Downs (also spelled Caroline), widow of Dr. E.M. Downs, held a meeting at her home on Main Street across from Pacific Street in December 1880 to organize the First Advent Christian Church of Tustin. Charter members included members of the Downs, Snow, Field, Hunt and Adams families.

They formed a committee and soon purchased property at the northeast corner of Pacific and Main Streets, the same location occupied by the church today. Hiram K. Snow was appointed head of the building committee that

The First Advent Christian Church was the first church to organize in Tustin. The chapel was completed in 1881 and is considered to be the oldest Protestant church in constant use by the same congregation in Orange County. It has been designated as an Orange County Historical Site. *Courtesy of Tustin Area Museum.*

set about to raise funds from the church members. The chapel, which is still in use, was completed in 1881, and a complete charter dated December 30, 1881, was issued by the County of Los Angeles. The building is considered to be the oldest Protestant church in constant use by the same congregation in Orange County. It has been designated as an Orange County Historical Site.

The Reverend Virgil F. Hunt was the first pastor, serving from 1881 to 1894. During 1881, the eighteen original members grew to forty-five members, including members of the Utt and Tustin families. Eventually a number of Irvine Ranch families, including the Williamses, Maynards and Searses, joined the congregation.

The sanctuary is now named Snow Memorial Chapel in memory of Dr. and Mrs. Downs's daughter, Cynthia, the first wife of Hiram K. Snow. Two of the original dark wooden pews brought around the Horn from Boston to San Diego, then to Tustin by wagon, have been in use since the dedication of the building on December 31, 1881, as has the clock, which the Reverend Hunt proclaimed would serve until the Lord returned.

Snow Memorial Chapel also is known for its antique pulpit settee and Lovers Window, as well as the display of the original charter. A memory corner exhibits a Medal of Honor awarded to James H. Brown, who joined the church in 1884, for service in the Civil War and a gold star for Edward Bristow, who lost his life in World War II.

The congregation has remained small and cohesive over the years. There have been several marriages between the founding families. Lucinda Elva Downs became the second wife of Hiram K. Snow after her older sister, Cynthia, died in 1880. Henrietta Downs married P.T. Adams.

The Tustin Presbyterian Church met at the Advent church until it completed its own church in 1884. Both the Episcopal and Methodist denominations had churches in Tustin in the early 1880s, but they did not last, although they reestablished themselves almost one hundred years later.

PRESBYTERIANS BUILD SANCTUARY

The residents of Tustin knew David Hewes as a wealthy Bay Area contractor and the man who furnished the golden spike for the completion of the transcontinental railroad, but they never dreamed that one day he would be their neighbor and benefactor.

But when Hewes and his wife, Matilda, who suffered from bronchitis, traveled to Southern California in June 1881, accompanied by her physician, in search of a climate favorable to her health, the couple selected Tustin after visiting various towns. They rented a home and made the move south. Franklina Bartlett, daughter of Mrs. Hewes, soon followed them with her husband, William S. Bartlett. The two couples bought property and built homes. The Hewes house still stands at the corner of Main and B.

Both families took part in the activities of Tustin. Hewes was the first president of the Santa Ana, Orange and Tustin Street Railway Company. He also served as president of the Santa Ana Valley Immigration Association, an organization formed to disseminate information concerning the advantages of the Santa Ana Valley and encourage immigration here. Mrs. Bartlett was instrumental in forming the Ebell Society.

Both Mr. and Mrs. Hewes had been active members of the Presbyterian Church of San Francisco, where Mr. Hewes served as a trustee. Neither Tustin nor Santa Ana had a Presbyterian church, although a small group met to worship occasionally in Santa Ana. By 1882, Hewes had organized a formal church with twenty-five members. The Reverend James H. Clark conducted services in Santa Ana in the morning and at a preaching station in Tustin in the afternoon.

Despite this arrangement, Mrs. Hewes felt Tustin needed its own Presbyterian church. Mr. Hewes later wrote, "Mrs. Hewes felt that the erection of this church would be of especial benefit to the young people of Tustin and that it would contribute greatly toward the future good of the place."

In 1883, Hewes bought a lot at the corner of Main and C and proposed that a church be built on it. Residents of Tustin raised $700. Friends of the Hewes family in San Francisco and Oakland contributed money and materials of various kinds. The steamer *Newport* arrived at Newport Beach, laden with windows, window frames, doors, shingles, lath, hardware and other materials for the new church. Hewes donated the church bell, which, following tradition, had once been used on a locomotive.

The church, built at a cost of $4,000, was dedicated in October 1884, with twenty-six charter members, including Mr. and Mrs. Hewes; Mrs. Mary Tustin, widow of Columbus Tustin; and their daughter, Mattie Tustin. Following a sermon preached by the Reverend Alexander Parker, Mr. Hewes, one of the first trustees, announced that he had assumed the payment of the

Tustin Presbyterian Church, which was built at a cost of $4,000, was dedicated in October 1884 with twenty-six charter members, including David and Matilda Hewes, who were generous contributors. The church was used until the present Mediterranean Revival–style sanctuary was built in 1929 for nearly $60,000. *Courtesy of Tustin Area Museum.*

small amount owing on the building and presented a deed to the church property "free and clear of all encumbrances."

When the Sunday school was organized, Hewes gifted it with a small library. Until her death in1887, Mrs. Hewes read every book that was added to determine its suitability for young readers.

The congregation continued to use the small wooden church until the present Mediterranean Revival–style sanctuary was built in 1929 at a cost of nearly $60,000.

Waterworks Establishes Home Service

The oldest business in Tustin, the City of Tustin Water Service, has survived three owners and three names and is still going strong after almost 125 years.

Early settlers depended on wells to provide water for their domestic needs, but in 1887, Charles F. and Hiram Willard and Henry Adams formed Willard Brothers Water Works to provide piped-in water to the homes in Tustin.

Utilizing an artesian well at the corner of Main and Prospect, they began to install pipes and expected to prosper with the boom of the late 1800s; however the business faltered when the boom fizzled out and a depression began in the mid-1890s.

Water was stored in the tank atop this structure at the Willard Brothers Water Works at the corner of Main and Prospect as part of the company's plan to install pipes to provide water from an artesian well to homes in Tustin. The high tower, called a tank house, offered a panoramic view of Tustin in 1887. *Courtesy of Tustin Area Museum.*

Adams left the firm, and Hiram Willard moved to Northern California. Charles Willard struggled with the losing venture until 1897, when he sold it to his former schoolmate, C.E. Utt, who paid him $2,000 for the business, which reportedly lost money for the next thirty years. Willard was said to have had a loss of more than $6,000.

Utt changed the name to Tustin Water Works and drilled a new well. To cut costs, he replaced the steam-driven pumps with gasoline-driven ones.

In Volume 1 of *History of Orange County* (Mrs. J.E. Pleasants, 1931), Utt wrote:

> *I, probably because I didn't know any better, took over the business and have operated it for 35 years. During this period, it has increased from 50 customers to 800, or from a losing business to a fairly profitable one.*
>
> *This increase cannot be taken as a gauge of population growth. A large part of it is due to the extension of the mains to include new territory. Now the old Willard Water Works serves a territory as large as the City of Santa Ana with only about one-tenth of the population.*

The Utt family operated the waterworks for over eighty years. Walter Rawlings, Utt's stepson, became superintendent and was in charge during the post–World War II growth in Tustin. New equipment and replacement buildings maintained the efficiency of the company.

The City of Tustin acquired the Tustin Water Works in 1982 as part of its Public Works Department, changing the name to City of Tustin Water Service.

RESIDENTS SUPPORT HORSE-DRAWN TROLLEY

It's been over one hundred years since the residents of Tustin City could jump on a streetcar and travel to Orange or Santa Ana. Granted, the trip was slow based on the speed of the mule or horse pulling the conveyance, but it was public transportation.

Three Tustin residents—David Hewes, Noah Palmer and Nelson Vanderlip, along with C.E. French, postmaster of Santa Ana—incorporated the Santa Ana, Orange and Tustin Street Railway back in January 1886. Records show that five hundred shares of capital stock were issued at ten dollars each. Hewes was named president of the company with Palmer as vice-president, Vanderlip as treasurer and French as secretary.

It was July before work was started on the installation of the steel rails with wood ties necessary for the streetcar tracks. Four months later, on November 23, 1886, the first streetcar pulled into Tustin City. The cars had been especially built, two open air and one enclosed. Each open car cost $1,350. The closed car cost a little more than $700.

Cars bound for Tustin City began their run at the corner of Fourth and Main in Santa Ana. Once passengers were aboard, the conveyance traveled south on Main to First Street, where it turned east. At Lyon, the route jogged south and after a short distance turned east onto Tustin's Main Street, which it followed into town. The journey to Tustin City was originally planned to end at the Tustin Hotel, a forty-room Victorian structure on Third Street between D (El Camino Real) and Prospect, but because of delays in completing construction of the hotel, passengers boarded and disembarked

The horse-drawn streetcar waits for passengers in front of the Bank of Tustin at the corner of Main and D (El Camino Real) in the late 1800s. The large building in back is the Tustin Hotel. The Utt home is seen in the lower right hand corner. *Courtesy of Tustin Area Museum.*

in front of the Bank of Tustin, later First National Bank of Tustin, at Main and D until the hotel opened in 1888.

Before waiting passengers could board the car for the return trip to Santa Ana, the horse had to be switched from one end to the other and the seat backs flipped. In Santa Ana, a turntable at the corner of Fourth and Main was used to turn the cars around. A man named Mr. Beebe drove the horse and collected fares.

Signs indicating the destination, Tustin, Orange or Santa Ana, were attached to the roof on both sides of each car. When not in use, horses and equipment were housed in a barn on West Fourth Street in Santa Ana.

The car was popular especially with the ladies who could use it when they wanted to shop or attend a meeting in Santa Ana, but when the economy slowed down in 1895 the line to Tustin was discontinued.

Roy Smith started running jitney buses from Tustin to Santa Ana about 1916. The vehicles, which were Model T Ford cars with the body lengthened to accommodate an extra seat, took about a half hour for a round trip. Fare was five cents. Percy Lusk bought this business about 1920. Millard Foster and his half brother, Scott Prather, acquired the company next and gradually added bigger buses.

The Orange County Transportation Authority now serves Tustin.

Construction Begins on Elegant Tustin Hotel

Developers in early Tustin had lots of big ideas, especially during the boom of the 1880s, but most of their projects failed. The Tustin Hotel is a good example.

In 1886, the Tustin Land and Improvement Company conceived the idea of building a grand hotel to attract tourists to Tustin. They bought two acres on Third Street between D (El Camino Real) and Prospect from Lysander Utt, paying him $2,000. Construction of a two-story, Victorian-style building, designed with Eastlake features by local builders George Preble and Chris McNeil, began within a short time.

In September 1887, a local Realtor, P.H. Look, purchased the uncompleted hotel for $20,000 with the understanding that the Tustin Land and Improvement Company would finish the construction. Three months later, Look sold the hotel to Sanford Johnson, who came to Tustin from Texas.

Everyone of any importance in Tustin turned out for the gala grand opening of the beautiful new forty-room Tustin Hotel in 1888. Little did the crowd realize, as they admired the grand staircase, magnificent lobby and beautiful chandeliers, that the operation was doomed to fail in five years. *Courtesy of Tustin Area Museum.*

No other building in Tustin equaled the structure, which had forty rooms reached by a grand staircase rising from a magnificent lobby with beautiful chandeliers. A broad front verandah overlooked a garden shaded by many trees. The Santa Ana, Orange and Tustin Street Railway Company's horse-drawn streetcar ended its run at the front entrance.

Johnson, who had brought black waiters, busboys and other employees with him from Texas, issued invitations for a gala grand opening in 1888. Tustin residents donned their finest clothes and enjoyed a festive evening, oohing and ahhing over its grandeur. When the hotel opened for guests, a tallyho made regular trips to the train depot in Santa Ana, hoping to pick up business for the hotel, but few people arrived who were interested in visiting Tustin.

The hotel struggled for five years, helped along by a loan from the Bank of Tustin. Johnson held a grand ball in 1893, but the hotel continued to fail. Johnson died in 1894, and the bank assumed ownership of the Tustin Hotel. The building changed hands several times and eventually became a boardinghouse.

The beautiful structure became a derelict eyesore with laundry hanging from the windows. The neglected garden was soon a weed patch. An advertisement in the January 1897 *Orange County Herald* offered the building for sale at a reduced price for use as a hotel, private school or sanitarium, but there were no takers.

The failure of the hotel had a direct effect on the Bank of Tustin. Although the loan was well secured at the time it was made, the death of Johnson and the resulting failure of the hotel were partially responsible for the bank having to close in 1902.

Twenty-five years after the gala grand opening, in 1913 C.Y. Martin, father of Glenn Martin, Orange County's aviation pioneer, was hired to tear down the building. Tustin's Wednesday Farmers Market is currently held on a portion of the property.

Library Opens in 1890

The Tustin Library has traveled a long and bumpy road with many stops since 1890, when a few Tustin ladies gathered a collection of books and set up a Reading Room in the Tustin Grammar School on C Street.

By 1906, more than 1,500 books were available to the school children and residents of Tustin. When the new Tustin Grammar School opened next door in 1914, the Reading Room, still staffed by volunteers, moved there.

The Orange County Free Library took over the Reading Room in 1924, opening it to the public, but branch service did not begin until 1931, when Mrs. Hazel Gowdy, wife of a Tustin orange grower, was hired as the first head librarian.

In 1933, an earthquake damaged the school, including the library. Temporary classrooms used up most of the vacant space in Tustin, but Mrs. Gowdy and the salvaged books found a home in a tiny office at the rear of the First National Bank building.

Carolyn Campbell, postmistress and library board member, called the new location that opened onto D Street (El Camino Real) "a miserable little hole." Her husband and several other men built temporary bookshelves, never dreaming that the library would stay in this cubbyhole until 1938.

Mrs. Gowdy and others in the community continually lobbied for better quarters, and the library finally was moved to a 1914-era building at 130 West Main Street. The chamber of commerce, businesses and individuals donated materials and money for tables, benches, magazine racks and shelves to equip this larger location. The Tustin High School shop classes under the direction of Orville Northrup, who would later become principal, volunteered as carpenters.

After the 1933 earthquake destroyed the portion of Tustin Grammar School that housed the Tustin Library, the books were moved to a tiny office between the entrance to the First National Bank of Tustin and Harry Pieper's Feed Store. Mrs. Hazel Gowdy, the librarian, was forced to stay in this "miserable little hole," as it was called, for five years. *Courtesy of Tustin Area Museum.*

In 1946, the library moved again—this time into the location now occupied by Rutabegorz. Then in 1950, they moved to the City of Tustin Annex on Third Street, sharing space with the fire department, police, city government and court.

Eight years later, the population growth forced another move to Andrews Street at Newport Avenue This building was enlarged in 1963 but soon became too small with a doubling of patron registration and tripling of circulation.

By 1974, the library no longer had room for its 59,304 volumes, including 32,438 adult books and 26,866 children's books, and plans were made for a 13,000-square-foot location in the yet-to-be-built Civic Center. Little did they realize when this proposal became a reality in 1974 that, years later, this space too would be outgrown and they would move again in 2009, this time into a light and airy 32,400-square-foot location with abundant comfortable seating and WiFi access throughout.

Other special features include an adult computer section, offering twenty-six computers and online catalog stations, nonfiction and fiction collections with large-print materials, a selection of two hundred magazines and newspapers, a teen "zone" equipped with six computers and study rooms, an adult quiet room, a computer lab for class-size instruction, a homework center, a community room and a large conference room, as well as space for the Friends of the Library book store.

The Elizabeth Anne MacPherson Children's Learning Center, featuring a story time room, study alcove, twenty computers, books to entice every child reader and a children's patio, is another gigantic plus.

FEW STORES IN EARLY TUSTIN

Early Tustin didn't offer many shopping opportunities. In 1890, a general store, a blacksmith shop and a drugstore pretty well took care of everyone's needs, according to an interview with William Martin Huntley in *Tustin Scrapbook*.

Most sources agree that the first drugstore opened about 1893 in Harlan Fairbank's real estate business building on the southeast corner of Main and D, but then opinions differ. Some say Fairbanks was a druggist as well a Realtor, as proven by a listing in the 1903 *Orange County Directory*. Others insist that Dr. Levi Fuller was the store's druggist.

Either or both could be right. You didn't have to have an education or a license to practice pharmacy around the turn of the century, according to William Soderlund, a fourth-generation pharmacist and curator of the William A. Soderlund Sr. Pharmacy Museum in St. Peter, Minnesota. "You just went into town, and if you did a good job, you stayed. If you killed off people, you didn't stick around too long. A guy could just put out a shingle."

Druggists concocted their own medicines, sometimes guided by a doctor's prescription. They also stocked the many patent medicines and cure-alls favored by mothers and housewives to treat illnesses.

About 1900, Tustin's drugstore moved west on the south side of Main Street to a location near the post office in the block between D and C. Carol Jordan's *Tustin: A City of Trees* refers to the wooden building, which also served as the Western Union Telegraph Office and Wells Fargo Express Office, as Dr. Levi Fuller's new drugstore.

This wooden-front store on West Main Street near the post office housed Dr. Levi Fuller's Tustin's drugstore, as well as the Western Union Telegraph Office and Wells Fargo Express Office, in the early 1900s. It was a favorite gathering place for the men of the community. *Courtesy of Tustin Area Museum.*

The 1908 *Orange County Directory* lists the site as the Tustin Drug Store at 719 East Main with Mary J. Meyers as manager. By the time the 1916 directory was published, the name had been changed to Tustin Drug Company with N.G. Walterhouse as proprietor. Around this time the drugstore appears to vanish following the tearing down of the building.

The Knights of Pythias constructed a new building with its lodge rooms over stores on the northeast corner of Main and D (El Camino Real) in 1925, and J.R. Harbour, who was elected city clerk when Tustin incorporated in 1927, soon opened a drugstore in the corner unit, adding a soda fountain that became a popular meeting place for the citizens of Tustin, both young and old. The next owner was Keller Watson, also owner of Watson's Drug Store in Orange, who called the store Watson's Drug Store No. 2.

Watson sold the store to Burt Muller and his brother-in-law, Bill Waters, at the beginning of the 1940s. They opened a variety store in the adjacent space on the north. The drugstore became a Rexall franchise with Rexall signs and products when Justin Dart took that brand name national in 1943.

Muller was the pharmacist and kept the store until 1950, when Glen Pyatt, a registered pharmacist with experience as a medic in World War II, bought both the drugstore and the variety store that could be entered from the drugstore. He closed the business after about twenty years when competition from the newly built shopping centers made it a losing investment. Old Town has been without a drugstore since that time.

Bicycle Becomes Popular Transportation

Bicycling became a popular method of transportation in Tustin and throughout the country after a bicycle with front and back wheels of nearly equal size and pedals connected to the rear wheel by a chain and sprocket was introduced about 1880.

Called the Safety—as opposed to the Ordinary, an earlier bike with a large front wheel and two small rear wheels—this bicycle was much easier to balance.

Pneumatic tires, coaster brakes and handlebars that could be adjusted added to its safety, as well as ease of riding. Manufacturers rapidly adopted the new design, and by the turn of the century, the fad of bicycle riding was booming.

Bicycling became a popular method of transportation and pleasure in Tustin after the Safety bicycle was introduced in 1880. Clubs were formed, and many men took part in bicycle races at the Santa Ana Bicycle Race Track, winning prizes donated by local merchants. Autos began to appear in the early 1900s. *Courtesy of Tustin Area Museum.*

Women soon joined men and children in riding the new machine for pleasure and transportation. They quickly discovered that bicycles required some changes in their clothing. Skirts became shorter and a few daring women tried the newly introduced trousers called bloomers. Susan B. Anthony declared in 1886 that bicycling had done more to emancipate women than anything else in the world, adding, "It gives a woman a feeling of freedom and self-reliance."

Bicycle riding became a sport and a way to get from one place to another. Clubs formed, with the Orange County Bicycle Club being the principal one in this area.

L.N. Crow was the proprietor of Tustin's first bicycle store on Main Street. Oscar Leihy later had the Tustin Cyclery on Main between C and D Streets. He and J.A. Hankey, the leading bicycle dealer in Santa Ana, were kept busy selling and repairing bicycles.

Tustin didn't tally the number of bicycles being ridden here, but Santa Ana claimed to have five thousand residents and two thousand bicycles.

A big bicycle race was held in 1889, using what was called a kite-shaped track. The cyclists started at First and Main Streets in Santa Ana, pedaling north to Chapman Avenue in Orange. Here they turned east to Prospect where they turned south, riding to First Street in Tustin, then traveling west to Grand Avenue where they turned north. After going west on Fourth Street, they crossed the finish line at French Street. Ralph Sutton and Percy Rice, both of Tustin, were among those winning prizes donated by local merchants. Sutton and another Tustin man, Ike Fields, frequently competed in races held at the Santa Ana Bicycle Race Track between Nineteenth and Twentieth Streets in Santa Ana.

Automobiles began to appear in Tustin in the early 1900s, but people continued to rely on bicycles. In 1899, about one million bicycles valued at more than $31 million were produced in the United States, but by 1909, the automobile had made the industry almost nonexistent.

Rice Family Introduces Culture

The Rice family was considered the epitome of success, wealth, sociability and culture in early Tustin.

James S. and Coralinn Rice, with their two young sons, James W. and Merrill, came to California from Cleveland, Ohio, in the winter of 1876.

Rice planned to join his brother-in-law, James Irvine, in raising cattle and hogs. The family moved into the Irvine's San Joaquin ranch house at the head of Newport Bay, but after a drought killed much of the livestock, they decided that ranch life was not for them.

In 1877, Rice bought fifty acres on the north side of First between Holt and Prospect in Tustin and built an ornate, three-story Victorian house that became the social center of Tustin after they moved in. A gentleman farmer, Rice first planted grapes and then oranges on the acreage surrounding the house.

Mrs. Rice, who was a gifted pianist and vocalist, soon became known as the Sweet Song Bird of Tustin. Rice was a talented whistler and often joined his wife in entertaining at lavish parties that they hosted. Their guests were the socialites of the area, including Mr. and Mrs. David Hewes, Madame Modjeska and Stella Nau.

Mrs. Rice and Madame Modjeska performed together several times in benefits held at French's Opera House in Santa Ana. Mrs. Rice drew large audiences of her friends when she appeared in the cantata *Esther*.

Percy Rice, the youngest son of James S. and Coralinn Rice, wealthy socialites in early Tustin, was an inventor from the time he was a young boy. He invented many zany items such as an automatic windshield wiper for spectacles, as well as useful items such as an automatic automobile shift and a push button radio tuner. *Courtesy of Tustin Area Museum.*

The Rices had two more sons after moving to Tustin, Harvey in 1878 and Percy in 1882. All four boys became well known in the community, and people marveled at how different each one was. Both James W. and Merrill inherited their parents' love of music. Harvey was a brilliant boy whose life ended with tuberculosis in 1900 at age twenty-one. Percy was an inventor from an early age.

When Percy was assigned the chore of caring for the family's flock of chickens each morning, he contrived a string and pulley arrangement for feeding and watering them without leaving his bed. After being spanked in school, he designed and built a spanking machine that he presented to Tustin superintendent of schools John Zielian.

James W. married Rubel Martin, and they had two children. Both a violinist and orange rancher, he built a large Victorian home at the corner of Seventeenth and Hewes.

Merrill became estranged from the family and left Tustin. According to local gossip, he was an early-day hippie who favored tattoos and a wild life.

Despite becoming a drunkard who was renowned for giving temperance speeches, Percy continued to be a successful inventor. His inventions covered a wide range, including a very successful automatic paper feed for printing presses introduced in 1903. Some of his inventions, such as the automatic windshield wiper for spectacles, were zany, but others proved valuable in industry. He invented an automatic gear shift for automobiles in 1913 and a push button tuner for radios in 1924.

Percy continued to visit in Tustin until his death in 1954. Coralinn and Merrill both died in 1919, James S. in 1939 and James W. in 1951. All were buried in Lawn K at Fairhaven Memorial Park.

Newcomers Build Beautiful Homes

When David Hewes and his wife, Matilda, came to Southern California in 1881, seeking a climate more beneficial to her bronchitis than the dampness of the San Francisco Bay area, they decided to settle in Tustin.

Hewes had made a fortune as a contractor in the city of the Golden Gate and achieved recognition for contributing a golden spike for California governor Leland Stanford to use in joining the final rails of the Transcontinental Railroad in the 1869 ceremonies. He was probably the wealthiest and most widely traveled man in Tustin at that time.

Soon after making their decision to move from San Francisco to Tustin, Mr. and Mrs. David Hewes bought property to build this Greek Revival/Italianate house at the corner of Main and B. The beautiful home is now considered a landmark, with a plaque designating it as an Orange County point of historical interest. *Courtesy of Tustin Area Museum.*

Soon after their decision to live in Tustin, Mr. and Mrs. Hewes bought property to build a home at the northwest corner of Main and B, now 350 B Street. No record remains of either the architect or the builder of the Greek Revival/Italianate house, which is constructed of redwood with square-cut handmade nails.

The entrance faces B Street with a wide wooden staircase leading to the double front doors that are accented by large plate glass windows in the top two-thirds and molding-trimmed paneling below. A porch with turned posts and balustrade runs across the front and extends back on both sides.

An amusing story—that may or may not be true—has been told over and over through the years. It seems that after she and her husband moved into the house, Mrs. Hewes was looking forward to being able to relax, rock and enjoy the front porch, but she soon discovered that her view was impaired by Fresnickers Saloon. After she complained to her husband, he solved the problem by buying the property occupied by the saloon and donating it to the First Presbyterian Church, along with money to build a sanctuary. Today, the church owns the entire block between B and C Streets.

After Mrs. Hewes died in 1887, Mr. Hewes continued to live in the house for several years before returning to San Francisco and remarrying. After he left Tustin, the house had a number of tenants, including Count Jaro Schmidt, who lived there in 1892. Benjamin F. Beswick, superintendent of Tustin Grammar School from 1919 to 1923, bought the house in 1916 and lived there until 1945.

Beswick, who firmly believed that all his teachers should live in Tustin, enforced this theory by remodeling the second floor of the house to provide bedrooms that he rented to them. This renovation altered the original roof line, but the house retained its architectural integrity.

The home continued to be a boardinghouse and became more and more dilapidated until the early 1950s, when it was sold. The buyers and future owners, including Linda and Steve Jennings, who have lived there for a number of years, have treated the house with loving care, restoring it to its original beauty and paying attention to detail with the best workmanship and materials.

The house is now considered a landmark, with a plaque designating it as an Orange County point of historical interest.

Lovely Home for Stevens's Bride

Probably no other residence in Old Town Tustin was owned by the same family for as many years as the home that Sherman Stevens built for his bride, Martha Snow, in 1887 at 228 Main Street.

After her husband died, Mrs. Stevens remained in the house until her death in 1948. At that time, their son, Horace, became the owner and kept the property until the late 1970s, when he sold it to Douglas Gfeller Construction Company, and it was turned into a business park.

Stevens, a wealthy businessman and a partner in the San Joaquin Fruit Company with C.E. Utt and James Irvine, hired two Los Angeles architects, Costerigan and Merithew, to design the Queen Anne cottage that was constructed of redwood shipped by boat from Eureka, California, to McFadden's Landing in Newport and brought to Tustin by horse and wagon. The home, lovely inside and out, stood among several acres of orange and avocado trees. An extensive garden of exotic plants and trees, as well as a habitat for animals collected by Stevens, surrounded the dwelling.

The garden housed a large aviary filled with exotic birds that Mr. and Mrs. Stevens, who were enthusiastic travelers, brought home from their travels around the world. Neighborhood children were welcome to visit the gardens and delighted in checking on the birds or hunting for brightly colored feathers.

Billy, a talkative parrot that lived in an orange tree, was well known for whistling at girls who walked down Main Street. Other popular residents in the garden included a bird of paradise, a golden cape pheasant, finches, canaries and many noisy parakeets. The children found a large loquat tree near the aviary an excellent perch for watching the birds and eating the tasty fruit.

Visits to the squirrel and the toucan cages were part of each trip to the gardens. Usually, one or both of the Stevens's two dogs—an Irish setter and a Gordon setter—tagged along with the children.

A tour of the garden always included the lath house, which was filled with exotic ferns and the cactus garden bordered with rocks and pieces of petrified wood. After being told about a child who fell into the cactus, the children were very cautious in this area. A colorful bed of purple violets, a

Although the Queen Anne cottage Sherman Stevens had built for his bride in 1887 is now part of an office complex, it is still surrounded by the palms and many other exotic trees and plants that filled the garden during the years it was their residence. Only the aviary, which fascinated the neighborhood children, is missing. *Courtesy of Tustin Area Museum.*

strawberry guava, a heliotrope and many camellia bushes were other "must sees" for the young visitors.

Lucky children who were invited into the house came out wide eyed, awed by the many treasures and the beautiful paintings collected by the Stevenses on their travels. Their extensive art collection is now housed at Bowers Museum in Santa Ana. The grand piano, possibly the only one in Tustin, the mahogany Victrola and the stack of National Geographic magazines, which they were encouraged to read, fascinated the youngsters.

Mr. and Mrs. Stevens, who were known for their generosity, also shared their garden with other Tustin children. Over the years, many Tustin teachers brought their classes to the garden and aviary on field trips.

The house, now part of an office complex known as Stevens Square, has been listed on the National Register of Historic Places since 1984.

Famous Opera Singer Joins Tustin Society

Although Madame Helena Modjeska lived in Tustin for only a few years in the early 1900s, she had many friends here and was an important part of the social scene. Known as Jadwiga Modrzejewsica Chlopowski, she was a premier actress in Poland until she decided to retire in 1875. After leaving the stage, she came to the Anaheim colony in 1876 with her husband, Karol Bozenta Chlopowski (Count Bozenta) and her son, Ralph. Supposedly leaving Poland to visit the Centennial Exposition in Philadelphia, they were really part of a small group of artists and writers who hoped to establish a utopian commune in the United States where they would be free of the restraints imposed in their homeland by Russian authorities.

They tried raising grapes in Anaheim but failed, leaving Count Bozenta in dire financial straits. In desperation, his wife went to San Francisco to learn English so she could return to the stage. Within six months, she was auditioning, and she soon made her American debut as Madame Modjeska, a name suggested by the manager of the California Theater.

After an enthusiastic welcome, she toured the United States and England for a number of years, appearing in productions such as *Camille*, *Henry VIII*, *As You Like It* and *Romeo and Juliet*. Theater greats such as Maurice Barrymore and Otis Skinner played opposite her.

Helena Modjeska, once a premier actress in Poland, retired when she came to the Anaheim Colony with her husband in 1876, but she learned English and returned to the stage after their grape-growing experiment failed. She had many friends in Tustin and rented a home here for several years in the early 1900s. *Courtesy of Tustin Area Museum.*

Despite her worldwide success as a Shakespearean actress, she still considered Orange County her home and returned as often as she could. In 1883, while spending the summer here with her husband and son, she purchased four hundred acres from J.E. Pleasants in Santiago Canyon. She commissioned Stanford White, a well-known architect who designed Madison Square Garden in New York, to design a ranch home for them. Today, the house, which is called Arden, is part of the Orange County Park system and is open to the public.

House guests such as Cornelia Otis Skinner and Ignace Jan Paderewski, as well as local residents, enjoyed her hospitality. Part of an elite group that included Tustin socialite Mrs. James Rice, Madam Modjeska often attended parties in Tustin and took part in amateur theatricals, in addition to appearing in benefit performances at French's Opera House in Santa Ana. She was loved by all who knew her, including James Irvine II, who named his daughter Helena in her honor.

In 1903, after she had retired from the stage for the second time, she performed for the Ebell Society of the Santa Ana Valley, presenting a program entitled *Loved Once* by Elizabeth Barrett Browning. The ladies made her an honorary member of the organization the next year.

Madame Modjeska sold Arden in 1906 and moved to Tustin, where she rented a home on West Main near Tustin Avenue. Called Los Alisos, it had been built for Roy "Cap" Ozmun and his wife and was said to be the largest one-story home in Orange County.

During her stay in Tustin, Madame Modjeska completed her memoirs with the help of author Constance Skinner. As her health began to fail, she decided that sea air would help her, and she purchased a small cottage on Bay Island in Newport Harbor from Sam Tustin. She lived there until her death on April 8, 1909. Her funeral was held at St. Vibiana's Cathedral in Los Angeles and she was buried in Krakow, Poland.

Murders Shock Community in 1889

Tustin residents gasped with alarm when they opened their copy of the *Santa Ana Blade* on Saturday morning, October 19, 1889, and read these words "Awful, Brutal, Butchery!—Cruel, Cowardly Crime!—of a Devilish, Damnable Demon!" Clutching the newspaper in disbelief, they continued to read that Mrs. O.R. Scholl of Tustin had cut the throats of her two young children and attempted to take her own life with muriatic and carbolic acids on October 16. The quiet, peaceful community was in an uproar.

How could a woman many of them knew—a churchgoer, a woman who lived in a cottage a short distance from her mother, Mrs. Mary Goodwin—

The early morning tranquility of tiny Tustin was shattered on the morning of October 19, 1889, and residents gasped in alarm as they read in the *Daily Blade*, a Santa Ana newspaper delivered to Tustin residents, the tragic news that Effie Scholl had cut the throats of her two children. *Courtesy of Tustin Area Museum.*

commit such a crime? It was true that she and her husband, Orlando R. Scholl, a grocer in partnership with George Edgar in Santa Ana, had divorced sometime earlier and he was now trying to regain custody of the children through Superior Court judge J.W. Ballard, his brother-in-law, as well as another Tustin resident, but was this reason for such a vicious action?

Skeptics pointed out that when her husband's health started to fail about a year after their 1883 marriage, he had left her to go to Northern California and work in the mines, an occupation he considered more healthful than being a grocer. Some felt relations were less than pleasant between the couple when he returned, causing him to file for a divorce that she contested.

Although Mrs. Scholl had been allowed to keep the children, neighbors said that her husband soon realized that she was unfit to keep and educate them and applied to the Superior Court for their custody.

Dr. John M. Lacy of Santa Ana, the family's doctor, was called when the murders were discovered early in the morning. After judging the situation, he returned to Santa Ana and summoned Dr. Avin Howe, Coroner E.D. Mills and Santa Ana constable George T. Insley to go back to Tustin with him. Because Tustin had no coroner or constable, these were officials elected by the newly formed Orange County.

Only the strongest could read the entire story as written by the *Santa Ana Blade*, but the gist was that Effie Scholl had been unsuccessful in killing herself after cutting the throats of the little boys whom she had first chloroformed. Dan Baker, editor of the *Blade*, printed and commented freely on the two letters that she had left behind for her mother and the coroner. His lurid descriptions were echoed by other Santa Ana papers, the *Free Press*, the *Standard* and the *Bulletin*, as well as the *Los Angeles Herald*.

Mrs. Scholl, who had been quoted as declaring to Coroner Insley that she would die and cheat the hangman of a job and disappoint some who would like to see her hanged, was true to her declaration. She died a few months later, and the incident was eventually forgotten.

The full story of Tustin's first murders, complete with every detail, may be read in *Turn the Rascals Out*, a biography of editor Dan Baker written by James Sleeper, a Tustin resident and well-known Orange County historian.

Chapter 3

Agriculture Develops

Acres of Apricots Are Planted

When the beautiful ornamental pear trees blossom in local gardens and parkways, I recall stories my mother told of the early 1900s when acres of apricot orchards near Tustin became bowers of pink and white flowers.

Tustin farmers had first planted grapes, but when a disease killed the vines, they replaced them with apricot trees. Eventually these trees lost out to orange and walnut trees, but for a time, apricots were an important crop in Tustin.

Two of the largest apricot groves in the county were located in Tustin. James Dunstan and his son, John, had twenty acres near the corner of Seventeenth and Yorba. James Ervin Luther harvested as many as seventeen tons of fruit from sixteen acres farther north on Yorba.

When the fruit was ripe, crews of local men, women and children came to work in what they called an apricot camp, moving from orchard to orchard until the harvest was completed. Large orchards required as many as forty workers.

Shady shelters were set up for the female workers, and although they kept busy, they had fun together. Owners often rewarded them for good work by taking them to the beach for a picnic when the season ended.

The drying process was primitive by today's standards. After the apricots were shaken from the trees to the ground by men using long poles, boys gathered them up into buckets that they carried to the women and girls.

Pitted apricots were dried naturally for market on large trays placed in open spaces between trees in the orchard. Crews of as many as forty workers, mainly housewives and young girls from the community, gathered in what was called an apricot camp and moved from orchard to orchard until the harvest was completed. *Courtesy of Tustin Area Historical Society.*

Their job was to split the fruit in half, remove the pit and lay the halves open side up on a drying tray.

The men carried the filled trays to the smokehouse and stacked them over a pan of sulfur that had been lit to burn slowly. The smoke helped the fruit retain its orange color and discouraged worms. After an hour or so, the trays were moved into the sun to complete the drying process. Within a few days the dried apricots were ready to be placed in bins where they stayed until sold to a wholesaler.

Apricots were marketed as both fresh and dried fruit, although sales of dried fruit were larger than those of the fresh fruit. The July 18, 1908 issue of Santa Ana's *Daily Evening Blade* newspaper reported that W.D. Bowman and Linneaus A. Cock, who each had ten acres of apricots in the Tustin area, were harvesting between four and five tons of fruit each day.

In 1910, 1.7 million pounds of dried apricots valued at $17,000 were harvested, as compared to $12,000 in fresh fruit sales. Total agriculture and horticultural production for Orange County in the same year was $12,294,694. The farmer often received as little as $0.01 a pound for his dried crop, but premium apricots could earn as much as $0.05 a pound.

Apricot growers joined with prune growers in 1917 and founded the California Prune and Apricot Association. Located in central California, the organization later adopted the name Sunsweet.

English Walnuts Replace Apricots

English walnuts were fast becoming a leader in Orange County horticulture in 1890, according to *An Illustrated History of Southern California*, published by the Lewis Publishing Company in Chicago.

Walnuts had been planted over a great portion of the vineyards devastated by the vine disease, and more walnuts than any other tree crop were planted during the past season, the article noted. No less than ten thousand acres were planted to walnut trees during 1889 with at least $50,000 worth of English walnuts from Orange County put on the market during the season. The publication estimated that fifteen thousand more acres would be planted in 1890.

"Orange County contains many thousands of acres particularly adapted for growing these nuts, and, as there is an unlimited demand for them at profitable prices, it is safe to predict that this will soon become the banner walnut producing county in California," the author concluded.

By 1919, California was producing more walnuts than any other place in the world. The entire state had 45,520 acres of walnut trees and produced 40,230,680 pounds of nuts. Orange County's share of this production was 12,358 acres, producing 15,849,000 pounds.

The next twelve years brought a decline in both trees and production. According to Farm Bureau figures, Orange County had 11,022 walnut trees in 1931. These produced 9,877,521 pounds of nuts and $1,724,216 in income. Farmers were discovering that although walnut trees were easy to grow, harvesting the crop was extremely labor intensive.

Walnuts were ready to harvest in late August or September when the bright green hull that encloses the nut began to split open. Men went into the orchard with long poles when this point was reached and shook the trees until the nuts that were ready fell to the ground. This procedure was repeated daily until the entire crop was off the trees.

Once the nuts were on the ground, crews of women and children combed the area, gathering the nuts into sacks and baskets. When the ground was clean, they sorted the nuts and removed any remaining hulls. Next they spread the nuts on trays to dry. The trays, which measured about three feet by six feet and had a depth of six inches, held about two sacks of nuts. After several days of seasoning in the sun, the nuts were resacked and taken to the packinghouse for winnowing (cleaning), bleaching, polishing, grading and sacking for market. Since Tustin had no walnut packinghouse, the local crop was sent to Santa Ana.

Large growers such as the Irvine Company hired itinerant workers to harvest their walnuts and set up housing camps in the orchards. Smaller growers relied on family members and neighbors to help with their harvests. Regardless, you could instantly identify anyone working the walnut harvest by the dirty, brown stains on their hands.

English walnut trees were planted as vineyards and apricot orchards failed, with at least ten thousand acres of walnuts planted in 1889. Although oranges eventually dominated, walnuts continued to be a profitable crop for more than thirty years. Walnut trees were easy to care for, but the harvesting of the nuts was labor intensive. *Courtesy of Tustin Area Museum.*

Although outranked by citrus production, walnuts continued to be a profitable crop for the next thirty-plus years. By 1965, both walnut and citrus growers were discovering that they could make more money with less labor by selling their land for housing tracts. Tustin no longer has walnut orchards, although a few homes have one or two trees left from earlier days.

Civil War Vet Emphasizes Oranges

Dr. William Burgess Wall, a medical doctor trained at Jefferson Medical College in Pennsylvania and a veteran of the Civil War, arrived in Tustin from Mississippi in 1875 and soon became the largest citrus grower in the area by purchasing and planting forty acres on the east side of Tustin Avenue.

One of the earliest and largest private citrus packinghouses in the Tustin area was owned by Dr. William Burgess Wall, *far left*, who came to the area in 1875 and planted at least forty acres of Valencia orange and lemon trees. In addition to being a physician, Dr. Wall was active in several agricultural organizations, including the Santa Ana Valley Irrigation Company. *Courtesy of Tustin Area Museum.*

This parcel extended eastward to the irrigation ditch that bisected the land between Yorba and Tustin Avenue and stretched almost to Seventeenth Street on the north. The Wall home, a beautiful, white, two-story house, was reached by a long drive entering from Tustin Avenue opposite Fruit Street. Today, Western Medical Center sits on a portion of the Wall property.

Dr. Wall planted the land surrounding the house and barn with Valencia, navel and lemon trees. Corrals and hog pens were located along the irrigation ditch. When the trees began to produce, he built one of the earliest and largest packinghouses in Tustin near the barn.

Dr. Wall became one of the first in Tustin to experiment with chemical sprays and gasses to kill the black, red and purple scale that infested the fruit. He tried different methods of applying these chemicals and soon learned that fumigating at night was the most effective.

Dr. Wall, who traveled to Tustin with a Mississippi friend, Dr. Paine, was soon joined by his wife, Julia. They had two children, William and Pearl. Mary, a daughter by his first wife who had died, also lived with them.

Dr. Wall was active in agricultural organizations and civic groups. He played a leading role in incorporating the Santa Ana Valley Irrigation Company to provide water to farmers in the Olive, Orange, Santa Ana and Tustin areas and served on the board for many years. He was also president of the Santa Ana Commercial Company and Orange Growers Association and a Tustin Sycamore School District Board of Trustees member from 1881 to 1883. When Orange County formed in 1889, Dr. Wall was appointed treasurer and served for two terms.

Despite his devotion to citrus ranching, Dr. Wall maintained a medical practice in Santa Ana and was one of the seven men who met to organize the Orange County Medical Association in 1889. He also served as the first president of the association.

A staunch Democrat, Dr. Wall attended a victory banquet for President-elect Grover Cleveland in 1892. During the evening, he admired a painting of a rooster that hung behind the head table and envisioned it as a label on his orange crates. When, at the end of the dinner, he approached the president-elect and told him that he would like to use it as his fruit label, Cleveland ripped the painting from the wall and handed it to him.

Dr. Wall registered the rooster label at the patent office and used it to identify his oranges until he closed his packinghouse and joined the Santiago Orange Growers Association (SOGA) operation in early 1900. After Wall died in 1909, his son sold all label rights to the SOGA for $50.

Since Julia had preceded her husband in death, William, Pearl and Mary were his only heirs. The two young women continued to live in the house after his death.

Many Young People Got Their Start in Oranges

The work was hard and the pay was meager, but for more than fifty years, Tustin's young people found their first jobs in the orange packinghouses.

After the orange growers organized a marketing group known as the Southern California Fruit Exchange in 1893, they formed local associations to pick, haul, pack and market their oranges. The Tustin area eventually had five associations—Tustin Hills, Golden West, Mutual Orange Distributors (MOD), Irvine Valencia and Francis Citrus—each with their own packinghouse and railroad spur.

Fruit was hauled from the orchards to the packinghouses on wagons pulled by teams of mules in the early years. Young men hired on as swampers (loaders) and drivers. Others worked at the packing plant, unloading fruit, guiding it through the packing process into precooling and cold storage plants and, eventually, loading market-ready boxes into railroad cars for shipment east.

Young women joined their mothers and other older women by the conveyor belts, plucking out the oranges and wrapping each one in tissue paper before adding it to the crate in which it would go to market. Each box was packed according to a specified diagram and inspected before it was market ready.

Although trucks eventually replaced wagons and teams and the packing process became more streamlined, lots of Tustin High School guys found their first job at a Tustin-area packinghouse. When those who still live in the area get together at a class reunion or some other event, their conversations often turn back to those hot summers when they hoisted boxes of oranges or jockeyed trucks weighted down with fruit.

They may recall veteran driver Shay Hansell as the old-timer who knew every orchard in the area and willingly helped the neophyte drivers. Or they may tell a story of how Grant Holderman, who had hauled oranges with a wagon and mules before any of their generation was born, had been called to bring his team into an orchard to do a job a truck couldn't handle.

In the early days of the citrus industry, men such as Fenlon C. Mathews, a Tustin citrus rancher, carried oranges from the orchard to the packinghouse on wagons pulled by teams of mules. The industry eventually became mechanized, and fleets of trucks driven by young men from the community came into use. *Courtesy of Tustin Area Museum.*

They laugh as they remember the minuscule pay, one dollar per hour for drivers and seventy-five cents per hour for swampers and how in the 1940s it paid for a lot of movie dates, dances at Balboa's Rendezvous, cars, gas and, in some cases, college.

Some shake their heads in amazement that the crazy guys they worked with actually became lawyers, school teachers and even Orange County deputy sheriffs. The banter becomes serious as they recall fellow workers who were killed in the war or have died.

Oranges are no longer important in Tustin, but the industry that provided the wherewithal for many young people is well remembered.

NEED FOR CITRUS PACKINGHOUSES DISAPPEARS

Tustin's many years as the hub of a profitable orange-growing empire drew to a close when the virus Quick Decline killed hundreds of trees in 1940. Before long, acres of orchards were being replaced by the houses needed to meet Orange County's rapid growth.

Soon Tustin's three citrus packinghouses were obsolete. Tustin Hills, the first to decide it could no longer continue operating, shut down in December 1963.

Tustin Hills had been organized as a cooperative by a group of growers in 1909. The packinghouse they built at that time on the Southern Pacific branch line between Holt and Newport near Irvine Boulevard was still being used at the time of the closure. The association was a member of the Southern California Fruit Exchange, a large marketing cooperative organized in 1895 in Los Angeles, which later became Sunkist.

About 300 growers belonged to Tustin Hills at its peak in 1945, according to a story in the January, 2, 1964 edition of the *Tustin News*. Only 138 remained to vote on it dissolution.

Closures continued with Golden West Citrus Association and Mutual Orange Distributors (MOD) ceasing operation within a few years. Golden West, which was established in 1917 to pack lemons, had branched into oranges and built a packinghouse on the east side of Newport Avenue south of Irvine Boulevard in 1930. The MOD packinghouse was on the west side of Newport between Main and Laguna Road.

All three packinghouses eventually were torn down but not before two earned moments of fame. The MOD packinghouse was renamed the Sunkist Cathedral and used by St. Cecilia's parish during the time their church on Sycamore was under construction. The Tustin Hills building became recognized as the locale for T. Jefferson Parker's *California Girl*, a

Three citrus packinghouses handled the orange and lemon crops grown in Tustin for many years until a virus killed the trees, and citrus orchards were replaced by housing tracts needed to meet the area's rapid growth. Tustin Hills, Golden West and Mutual Orange Distributors packinghouses closed and were eventually torn down. *Courtesy of Tustin Area Museum.*

murder mystery. Parker was familiar with the site from the years he had lived in Tustin and attended Tustin High School.

The earliest orange packinghouses in Tustin were independent ones built in the late 1880s by citrus growers with large acreages. Dr. William B. Wall probably ran the largest, but A. Guy Smith, Nelson Vanderlip and H.C. Snow also packed their own fruit. H.W. Judson was the first to organize the growers in his neighborhood into a cooperative.

After the Santa Ana Valley Fruit Company organized in 1885 and shipped more than one hundred cars of oranges from Santa Ana on the Southern Pacific line, growers became more interested in the benefits of companies or cooperatives handling the shipping and marketing of their fruit. The invention of the refrigerated rail car in 1890 by Edwin T. Earl facilitated the shipment of oranges to the eastern market. Tustin Packing Company opened in 1905 in an old warehouse near the Southern Pacific depot, but it lasted only a short time.

The Southern Pacific line continued to carry oranges packed by all three Tustin packinghouses to Los Angeles until it was washed out by a flood in 1969.

COLORFUL LABELS IDENTIFY ORANGE CRATES

As a child I had no idea that the oranges from our orchard eventually traveled to market in wooden crates with colorful labels. The field boxes that were unloaded in our orchard the day before the pickers arrived were the only boxes I ever saw. Stenciled with the name of the packinghouse, these heavy wooden boxes took a lot of abuse.

When orange growers, such as Dr. William Burgess Wall, who packed and shipped their own fruit in the early years, found the baskets and barrels customarily used to ship fruit were unsatisfactory for sending oranges east by railroad car, they developed a lightweight wooden orange crate for marketing.

Manufactured in a rectangular shape, twenty-seven inches by twelve by twelve, with a slatted lid, this box was durable and attractive, as well as easy to handle and load quickly into a railroad car. Wooden crates were used from the late 1800s until the 1950s, when they were replaced by cardboard boxes.

In the beginning, the name of the packinghouse and the grade of the orange packed inside was stenciled on each crate. Although this identification was sufficient, it was not especially attractive and had little appeal for the wholesalers who bought the oranges. As a result, a colorful ten by eleven inch label was designed to attract attention and promote the product.

Designed by commercial artists, most of these labels were produced in San Francisco and Los Angeles. Gordon T. McClellan and Jay T. Last, authors of *California Orange Box Labels*, estimate that there were eight thousand label designs at the peak of the orange industry in California. With adaptations, this resulted in fifteen thousand labels.

The label designs changed over the years. From 1880 until after World War I, labels featured flowers, birds, animals and scenic views with a few historic themes. By 1920, the labels switched to stressing the health benefits of oranges and orange juice. From 1930 until the mid-1950s, when the cardboard carton came into use, label designs used more lettering and geometric shapes than illustrations.

Label production ended abruptly in 1955 when the rising cost of wood forced packinghouses to switch to cardboard cartons for shipping. Simple designs were printed on the box ends, ending the need for the colorful labels. Thousands of unused labels were thrown out or stashed in basements of the packinghouses.

More than eight thousand label designs such as this were used to identify the various brands of oranges packed at the peak of the citrus industry. Label production ended in 1955 when the industry switched from wooden crates to cardboard cartons. Now the unused labels are valued as collector items, bought from shops or on the Internet. *Courtesy of Tustin Area Museum.*

Stone lithography was used to produce the early labels. Later, photo composition and offset printing came into use. Surprisingly, few artists signed their designs. Probably no one ever thought that in later years orange crate label collecting would become popular.

Because it is virtually impossible to remove a label from an old crate, labels from the early years are rare, but there are many unused labels available at nominal cost. Collectors trade and sell their labels or buy from shops or on the Internet. A number of books have been written on the subject.

Prices range from low to high, depending on supply and demand. Strangely, orange crate labels are collected for the role they played in the history of advertising rather than their contribution to the citrus industry.

PESTS PLAGUE GROWERS

The first orange orchard in the area that would become Orange County was planted in Orange in 1873 by Patterson Bowers. In 1876, Dr. W.B. Wall planted an orchard on the east side of Glen Avenue (now Tustin Avenue) in Tustin. Sam Preble, Columbus Tustin, Charles Wheaton Wilcox, Hiram K. Snow and P.T. Adams soon followed his lead.

According to the *State of California Gazetteer*, published by R.L. Polk & Company in 1888, "Oranges were one of the principal crops around Tustin in the boom days of 1887–88."

Growers were troubled by pest infestations from the very first. Black scale was thought to have been introduced into the area on trees brought from Los Angeles. Red scale, which is capable of doing great damage to orchards, made its presence known around 1884 and 1885. Again, Los Angeles was blamed as the culprit since growers believed that trees purchased from T.A. Garey carried the pest. Navel stock brought from Australia shared the blame, as did the San Gabriel area, where red scale was first discovered.

Orange growers tried several means of eradicating the pests that threatened the orchards and the future of the citrus industry. Spraying was tried in 1882, using fish oil as a base for carrying a caustic chemical. Although used widely, this wash brought few benefits and many negatives. The alkali in the treatment damaged both the trees and the fruit.

A.D. Bishop, a citrus grower in Orange, developed a spray called a raisin wash in 1885. This was widely used for several years. Although the division of entomology of the Department of Agriculture in Washington, D.C., sent special agents to the county periodically, no successful way to destroy the citrus pests was developed. Black and red scale continued to menace the industry.

A breakthrough came in 1889 when Bishop developed a method of destroying scale by covering the trees with canvas tents and fumigating with a gas made from cyanide of potassium and sulfuric acid. Despite some burning of the trees and fruit, this proved to be the most effective method of destroying scale to date.

A number of experiments were conducted after less damage was noted when fumigation was done on cloudy days. Decreasing the amount of light by painting the canvas tents black proved mildly successful. Then Tustin growers Dr. W.B. Wall and Moses S. Jones discovered that fumigating at night when the temperature was cooler produced better results. Joining with Bishop, they took out a patent on night fumigation and offered the method to the county for $10,000. The board of supervisors failed to approve the deal, and the courts soon annulled the patent on the grounds that darkness

After lots of experimentation, early growers learned to control pest infestations in the orange groves by using sprays and fumigation. Later companies formed to handle this work for growers and were profitable businesses until the decline of the citrus industry. Graves & Howley were among the most successful. *Courtesy of Tustin Area Museum.*

could not be patented. Fumigation continued for many years, with A.E. Bennett, Charles Bowman, N.F. Ritchey and Benjamin Aldridge operating the earliest agricultural pest-control businesses. Eventually, a successful method of spraying was developed and replaced most fumigation. William Graves, George Howley, Robert P. Buckner and Paul Andres became familiar names in the business that thrived as long as the citrus industry had a foothold in Tustin.

SMUDGE POTS PROTECT TREES ON COLD NIGHTS

Back in the days when Tustin was a valuable citrus producing area, growers worried that January's cold, cloudless, windless nights would bring freezing temperatures, damaging the trees and the fruit.

The method used to keep the orchards warm was a refinement of the practice of burning brush and tree trimmings that began back in the late 1880s. By 1910, growers were using smoke created by burning fuel oil.

Smudge pots filled with coke, a high carbon content fuel, were set out between the orange trees. When ignited, they produced heat and a veil of greasy, dark smoke that kept the trees warm during cold nights of twenty-eight degrees or lower temperature. They were eventually replaced by oil reservoirs with pumping systems and wind machines with huge propellers. Snow shown here was a rare phenomenon in 1949. *Courtesy of Tustin Area Museum.*

The smudge pots they eventually used to line the aisles between the trees looked like upside-down mushrooms. Each pot had a squatty, sheet-metal base, about twenty-four inches in diameter and twelve inches deep, with a removable chimney about two feet high. In anticipation of the temperature dropping to twenty-eight degrees or lower, workers filled the pots with coke, a fuel with high carbon content distilled from coal or oil. Each pot held enough coke to provide eight hours of warmth.

Growers made sure that they never missed the nightly frost broadcast during the winter months. With this as a warning, they were prepared to go into action when the siren atop the First National Bank building sounded to announce the temperature drop.

Workers, usually hired hands and high school boys, used this siren as a signal to report for work. Bundled against the cold in boots, heavy jackets and hats, they would trudge through rows of trees, lighting each pot with a torch. The rest of the night was spent watching the thermometer and checking the pots.

In the late '30s, some growers replaced smudge pots with oil reservoirs and pumping systems that carried fuel to burners located permanently among the trees. Although this eliminated the job of refilling the pots with coke after they had burned all night, each burner still had to be ignited. Wind machines and huge propellers came later. Requiring less labor, these devices prevented frost by providing air circulation.

The orchards glowed with an eerie orange light during a night of smudging. A veil of greasy, dark smoke hovered over the trees and as far as the eye could see when it grew light.

Anyone venturing outside, including kids waiting for the school bus or walking to school, soon had black-rimmed nostrils. Holding a handkerchief or scarf over the mouth and nose helped a little.

Housewives detested smudging. Efforts to keep the sooty mess out of the house were futile. White curtains turned dingy, piano keys yellowed, oil film settled on all surfaces. Floors were discolored as shoes carried in soot.

The dirty air created by smudging did not readily disperse. Even if temperatures remained above freezing in Tustin, the results of smudging in orchards in Placentia, Fullerton, Anaheim and as far away as Pomona would drift in as the day advanced. This would be considered a health problem today, but at the time it was accepted as part of the process of growing oranges.

Smudging was neither cheap nor 100 percent effective. After paying fuel and labor expenses, a grower could still have a damaged crop and lost income. Citrus growers debated the value of trying to keep the orchard warm, but there was always the hope that this would be the year that the fruit survived the cold.

UTT PLANTS GRAPES, CHILIES, PEANUTS

Rancher, developer, businessman, civic leader and man of much enterprise were some of the terms used to describe the career of Tustin's Charles Edward Utt, better known as C.E. or Ed.

Coming to Tustin with his parents, Lysander and Emily Arvilla Utt, at the age of eight, he completed Tustin Grammar School and worked at an assortment of jobs until his father died, leaving him in charge of the L. Utt Pioneer Store in 1891. He managed the store for about two years before selling it and ending his merchandising career.

In 1896, he bought the floundering waterworks from the Willard Brothers and eventually turned it into a successful operation, which he renamed Tustin Water Works. His stepson, Walter Rawlings, eventually took over the management, but Utt remained part of the operation. The City of Tustin purchased the waterworks in 1982.

Utt served on the board of directors for Tustin's first bank, Bank of Tustin, which opened in 1888 and closed in 1902. When the First National Bank of Tustin opened in 1911, he served on the board of directors and later became president.

A great believer in education, Utt served on the Tustin Grammar School District Board and played a prominent role in the organization of the Tustin Union High School District. C.E. Utt Middle School recognizes his contributions to education.

Utt began his agricultural career with Sherman Stevens in 1906 and soon became known as one of Orange County's most progressive agriculturists. The two leased one thousand acres from James Irvine and organized the San Joaquin Fruit Company. After they planted Valencia oranges, lemons and walnuts on the property, Utt introduced the practice of growing beans, peanuts and chilies between the rows until the trees came into production.

Around 1914, Utt planted a vineyard on Lemon Heights where he had built a home. The abundance of grapes produced on this acreage led him to another business adventure, The Utt Juice Company. After bottling grape juice on his back porch for several years and giving it away to family and friends, Utt expanded the operation and moved into a building that he owned at the corner of Prospect and Main. Arcy Schellhous soon joined him as a partner in establishing the Queen Isabella brand of juice, jams and jellies. They added pomegranate, rhubarb and guava juice to their inventory. Schellhous bought out Utt in 1931, although the company continued to use the Utt name.

Production reached a peak of 200,000 gallons of juice in 1965. The company was ahead of its time in producing juices that could be labeled "100% Pure, No Sugar Added." Boysenberry products that carried the Knott label were also manufactured.

Schellhous continued to run the company until he died in an automobile accident in 1970. Jack Hall, who had joined the company in 1946 as office manager, became president and served until 1973 when a scarcity of fruit and increasing competition forced the company to close. It was calculated that Utt's back porch venture eventually produced seven million gallons of juice.

Utt was one of the first to plant peanuts and chilies as crops in the Tustin area. Soon he was producing many sacks of peanuts for the market and

Utt Grape Juice Company produced juice, jams and jellies in downtown Tustin for many years. Founder C.E. Utt had numerous other agricultural and business interests in addition to serving on several bank boards and both Tustin Grammar School and Tustin High School boards. C.E. Utt Middle School recognizes his service to education. *Courtesy of Tustin Area Museum.*

became known as the Peanut King. He also gained recognition by inventing a chili dry house to replace the method of curing peppers by laying them in the sun to dry. Although not as picturesque as the colorful strings of red peppers reflecting the sunlight, the drying shed was much more efficient.

Eventually the San Joaquin Fruit Company used its experience gained on the Irvine Ranch to develop property in Ventura County. Utt formed the Utt Development Company in Oxnard, California, and developed ranches in the Simi Valley and Point Magu areas.

It was said that Utt, who died in 1951, had grown every major crop possible in Orange County with the exception of sugar beets.

HAVEN SEED COMPANY MOVES TO TUSTIN

Because this area still had a fair amount of land available for agriculture, the Haven Seed Company decided to locate its business in Tustin when it made a move to Orange County from Arroyo Grande and Lodi in 1910.

The company, which was once recognized worldwide, was started in 1875 by Edwin M. Haven in Bloomingdale, Michigan. In 1903, he moved to California where he grew tomatoes for seed on leased land in Arroyo Grande and Lodi. Settling in Tustin, the company increased the amount of acreage that the seed farm planted each year.

Archie and Lawrence, the two older sons, joined their father in the business that incorporated as Haven Seed Company in 1914. When the business outgrew the acreage available in Tustin, the Havens moved the operation to forty acres that they purchased near Edinger and Flower, just outside Santa Ana's southern boundary.

When they arrived in Tustin, Edwin Haven, his wife and their eight children moved into a small house they rented from David Cobau at 639 West Main Street. This Victorian Italianate cottage is now identified as the Leinberger house. They later moved into the Hewes House at the corner of Main and B and lived there until Mr. Haven passed away in 1917. At that time, Mrs. Haven and the children still living at home moved to Santa Ana.

Archie, who married a Tustin girl, Lizzie H. Brown, in 1911, and Lawrence, husband of Cammie B. Mitchell, took over the operation of the seed company as president/general manager and secretary. C.E. Utt, a successful Tustin businessman, entrepreneur, and agriculturist, became treasurer.

Workmen prepare to harvest seed from peppers grown by the Haven Seed Company. This company, which did outstanding work in the breeding of both tomatoes and peppers and produced seed for the wholesale trade and mail order houses, had acreage in Tustin. Owner Edwin M. Haven and his family also lived in Tustin, with the children attending Tustin schools. *Courtesy of Orange County Historical Society.*

The company prospered, developing new varieties of tomatoes and bell peppers and shipping seeds all over the world, thus earning Santa Ana the unofficial title of "Tomato Seed Capital of the World."

A younger son, Bill, was born in 1901, attended Tustin Grammar School and graduated from Santa Ana High School. After he joined the firm, he became vice-president and sales manager.

His wife, Vera M. Clapp, a Santa Ana High School classmate, recalled in her memoirs that "he was successful in improving the strains of several tomato varieties and Haven tomato seed was known the world over in the wholesale trade and mail order houses as the world's best."

Bill also developed a heavy thick-meat bell pepper known as the California Wonder. Because of his outstanding work in the selective breeding of tomatoes, as well as the development of several booklets cataloging over ninety varieties of tomatoes, he was elected to the board of the Western States Seedmen's Association and became chairman of the Growers Division.

Despite his work, the company faltered after the 1930s and closed in 1946, according to records stored in the archives of the Orange County Historical Society.

Chapter 4

First World War Slows Growth

Early Autos Come to Tustin

There's a lot of disagreement as to which Tustin resident bought the first automobile, but one thing is certain: he or she had to be wealthy.

As 1899 rolled into 1900, automobiles were a novelty that could be enjoyed only by the very rich. Most people still used the horse and buggy or a bicycle to get around town and a train for long distances. Many believed the automobile would never catch on. "Get a horse" was often heard, especially when a driver was struggling with a flat tire or other problem.

Horatio Augustus Allen, who bought an EMF, certainly qualified as one of the wealthiest men in Tustin. He owned eighty acres—all planted with walnuts with the exception of fifteen acres of Valencia and navel oranges. EMF was produced in 1908 by Wayne Motor Company, which had merged with Northern Motor Car Company. The four-cylinder, five-passenger car sold for $1,250.

Roy "Cap" Ozum, the wealthy yachtsman who built his Los Alisos estate on Main Street near Tustin Avenue in 1902, was known for his stable of fine horses, each with its own groom. But when the automobile bug bit him, he sold the horses, turned the barn into a garage and hired mechanics to keep his autos in top shape. Mrs. Ozum drove a bright red roadster and scandalized the locals as she raced along Tustin's dusty roads.

Martha Preble, wife of J.O. Preble, also was driving her own car in Tustin in 1912. A socialite and a musician who belonged to the Ebell Society and

An early car owner, First National Bank of Tustin cashier C.A. Vance frequently took his wife and two daughters for a spin in his new touring car. Only a few Tustin residents acquired cars in the early 1900s, but by the 1920s, cars ranging from an electric coupe to Buick touring car were a common sight on the streets and Tustin's first garage had opened. *Courtesy of Tustin Area Museum.*

Santa Ana chapter of Eastern Star, she drove alone in a small, two-cylinder, one-seat Maxwell. The popular Maxwell was manufactured from about 1904 to 1925. By 1914, the company had sold sixty thousand cars.

Martha Stevens, wife of Sherman Stevens, was another early female driver. She had the only electric car in Tustin. The shiny black coupe that was steered by a tiller, rather than a wheel, was kept in the Stevenses' carriage house.

Porter Luther, son of James Ervin Luther, an apricot and citrus grower with a ranch on Yorba Street, had a sporty Hupmobile roadster. Sam Nau and John Dunstan were other citrus growers who bought automobiles early on.

Sam Tustin bought a Buick touring car in 1915, but he often left it in the shed where he stored it. An amusing, supposedly true story says that one day a man asked Sam why he was riding his bicycle instead of driving his Buick, and Sam replied that he was in too big of a hurry to get it out of the shed. Regardless, he eventually donated the car to the Tustin Chamber of Commerce, and it was converted into a firetruck for the volunteer fire department. The vehicle, which served for many years, is now in the Tustin Area Museum.

Sensing a need in Tustin around 1913, Robert J. Wiley constructed the building that is still in use at the corner of Third and C Streets and opened an agency for Chalmers Motor Car Company, located in Detroit. Chalmers were expensive cars for the period, perhaps too expensive since, by 1915, Wiley had sold the building to William Huntley and Nick Gulick, who opened Tustin's first garage there.

Henry Ford changed the status quo when he started manufacturing the Model T. By the 1920s, cars were a common sight on the Streets of Tustin.

CHAMBER OF COMMERCE ORGANIZES FIRE DEPARTMENT

Correspondence between the Tustin Fire Department and the American La France Fire Engine Company in San Francisco in 1915 is the first record of the existence of a fire department thought to have been organized by the chamber of commerce.

Apparently their interest in buying equipment came to naught because the volunteers continued to pull a forty-gallon chemical tank mounted on two large wheels to fires, according to the late Will Huntley who owned the tank and stored it at his Tustin Garage. Pushed or pulled by several men or towed behind an automobile, this was a cumbersome piece of equipment.

But it continued to be used until about 1924 when Sam Tustin, son of Columbus Tustin, donated his 1912 Buick touring car to the chamber of commerce. As Huntley remembered in a 1964 *Tustin News* story, the vehicle was sent out of town to be converted into a firetruck with two copper tanks. One tank held soda and one held acid. A former fire chief, Pete Riehl, recalled in the same story that "many a fireman went home with holes in his clothing after reloading the tank with sulfuric acid."

The first organizational meeting of the Tustin Fire Department was held that same year in the Knights of Pythias hall. Thirty-two men signed up as volunteers. Tustin had a population of five hundred and an area of 0.31 miles.

Two events that year brought changes to the fire department. First, a siren was purchased and installed on top of the First National Bank building at the corner of Main and D (El Camino Real). The operator in the telephone exchange that occupied space in the building was responsible for sounding the alarm, which called out the volunteers. Second, Tustin citizens voted to incorporate and elected a city council that included four volunteer firemen, Charles Logan, fire chief; William Huntley; Edmond Kiser; and Fred

After years of manually pulling a forty-gallon chemical tank to fires, the Tustin Volunteer Fire Department acquired a vehicle in 1924 when Sam Tustin donated his 1912 Buick touring car to the chamber of commerce, which had it converted into a firetruck. William Huntley stored the vehicle in his Tustin Garage and usually drove it assisted by Nick Gulick. *Courtesy of Tustin Area Museum.*

Schwendeman. In May 1928, the city council voted to take over the fire equipment and began paying part of the expense for items such as caps, coats and state insurance for the fifteen volunteers.

In 1930, the community voted favorably for fire bonds, 134–10. This allowed the city to build a fire station to house the equipment and purchase a second firetruck, a Seagrave five-hundred-gallons-per-minute pumper. The new station had facilities to accommodate as many as five volunteers at night.

Additional equipment was acquired as the population and area of Tustin expanded, but the fire department continued to be staffed by volunteers with little or no training until 1963, when the first examination for paid firemen was held. Three firemen, all former volunteers, were hired. A second examination was held the next year, and two more paid firemen were added. The city continued to acquire more fire equipment, two new stations and paid firemen. By 1977, fire personnel consisted of a chief, two battalion chiefs, six captains, six engineers, twelve full-time firemen, one volunteer and ten explorers.

Despite the growth of the department, it was decided that it would be more efficient to contract fire services out to the Orange County Fire Authority, which assumed responsibility on January 1, 1978, ending an era of more than fifty years.

LUMBER YARD HAS LONG LIFE

In all the years of Tustin's existence, few businesses have lasted as long as or with less competition than the Tustin Lumber Company, which, despite several changes in name, endured for eighty-three years.

S.E. Tingley and his wife, Sara, came to Orange County from San Diego in 1902 and settled in Santa Ana where he became a salesman for the Pendleton Lumber Yard on East Walnut. Eight years later, Tingley went out on his own and established Tustin Lumber Company on East Main in Tustin near the Southern Pacific Railroad depot on Newport Avenue.

He built a lumber shed with office facilities and was soon picking up deliveries of lumber that arrived at the depot. Business thrived, and he was able to expand the yard with additional buildings. His only competition was a branch of Pendleton Lumber Company, which opened in 1916 at the corner of Newport and Laguna Roads and operated for a short time.

The Tingleys and their daughter, Margaret, who later became Mrs. Lee Byrd, lived on D Street between Third and Main Streets. They were active members of the Tustin Presbyterian Church. Tingley was a member of the building committee when the new church was built in 1929 and served several terms as trustee. He also was active in the chamber of commerce and the Masonic Lodge.

By 1926, Tingley was able to move the Tustin Lumber Company to a large Spanish Revival–style building that he had built on the curve where D Street (El Camino Real) dead ended at First Street. The handsome building had showrooms and storage for building materials. Murals depicting homes built in styles popular at that time decorated the front of the building with several arched entrances.

Writing in *The History of Orange County* in 1916, Samuel Armor described the business as playing an important part in the development of the area.

> *They do a general lumber and mill business and handle all kinds of builders' materials, cement, roofing and wall board, and by anticipating the wants rather than merely catering to the needs of the community, render the town and environs a great service. A large force of men is employed on the two acres of the company, and it is not surprising that their business last year amounted to $40,000.*

Despite its success, the company became Whitson Lumber Company, a branch of a Santa Ana lumber company owned by W. Verne Whitson in 1931. Although Tingley died in 1942, the business once more became Tustin Lumber Company in 1947, with A.C. Hutchison as manager.

Tustin Lumber Yard, which opened in 1910 near the depot on Newport Avenue, moved to this location in 1926. The only lumber yard in Tustin with the exception of a short time in 1916 when Pendleton Lumber Company was open, the business provided all kinds of building materials and remained successful until the arrival of Home Depot and other "big box" home centers. *Courtesy of Tustin Area Museum.*

The name changed to Mullin Lumber Company of Tustin in 1956, and Don A. Taylor assumed managerial duties. This lasted until 1968 when the lumberyard once more became Tustin Lumber Company. This name stayed on the building until it was torn down in 1993.

Records fail to show who owned the lumber yard in the years after 1947 when the business returned to the Tustin Lumber Company name. One can only speculate that perhaps Tingley's heirs assumed ownership after his death and possibly leased out the business. Regardless, it was successful until the arrival of Home Depot and other "big box" home centers.

FIRST NATIONAL BANK REPLACES DEFUNCT BANK OF TUSTIN

The Bank of Tustin and its successor, the First National Bank of Tustin, were the community's only financial institutions for over seventy years—in sharp comparison to the dozen or more now serving the area.

A. Guy Smith served as president of the Bank of Tustin. Other directors were Noah Palmer, vice-president; Edwin D. Buss, cashier; Charles W. Wilson; W.S. Bartlett; H.F. Kendall; Sam W. Preble; W.W. Martin; and C.E. Utt. They built a handsome, two-story building in the Richardsonian Romanesque style of architecture on the northwest corner of Main and D (El Camino Real) and opened for business about August 1, 1888.

The bank survived the Panic of 1893, only to close its doors in 1902 due to what the former cashier called three mistakes. First, they spent too much money on their elaborate headquarters. Second, the small amount of authorized capital was not paid up. And third, they loaned a large sum of money to the Tustin Hotel, which failed when its owner, Sanford Johnson, died unexpectedly.

In direct contrast, the First National Bank of Tustin was successful from the day it opened on December 20, 1911. Organized as a member of the Federal Reserve Board, its volume of business grew from its inception, and judicious management soon increased its capital to $50,000, with deposits of over $400,000.

W.C. Crawford was the first president; John Dunstan was vice-president. The board included Sherman Stevens, C.E. Utt, Victor Tubbs and Rufus Sandborn. C.J. Cranston was the first cashier.

The bank prospered under Cranston. In 1917, he sold his shares and position, as well as his house, to C.A. Vance, a newcomer to Tustin. A native of Kansas, Vance had owned a bank there that he sold in 1912 and moved to Chula Vista, California, where he organized the Chula Vista State Bank. He sold this bank in August 1916, and on January 1, 1917, relocated to Tustin with his family, settling into a large Victorian house on Main a few blocks west of the business area.

William S. Leinberger, who came to California in 1910 from Nebraska and worked at the Alhambra Savings Bank, was hired as assistant cashier about the same time. He also bought a home on Main Street. These two men were said to "display their knowledge of the banking business in a creditable manner."

In 1933, when Franklin D. Roosevelt declared a bank holiday to end a run on banks by the depositors, Vance closed the front doors in compliance with the president's edict; however, he continued to do business from the back door in the alley, and the community was able to brag that the First National Bank of Tustin never closed during the dark days of the Depression.

The First National Bank of Tustin was successful from the day it opened in 1911. A replacement for the unsuccessful Bank of Tustin, it was the town's only bank for many years. With the same staff for almost its entire existence, it survived three robberies, including one in which the culprit was shot. *Courtesy of Tustin Area Museum.*

Vance and Leinberger—with the help of Frances Logan, who joined the bank as a teller shortly after they were hired, and Vance's son-in-law, G.O. Bixler, who was hired later—ran the bank successfully. The building lost its turret and other architectural features in the 1933 earthquake, and the employees survived at least three robberies, including the last one in which Bixler shot the culprit, but little else changed. The First National Bank of Tustin was a successful and important part of the community until it was purchased by First Western in 1959.

Fearing another earthquake, bank officials moved the branch several doors north into a new building. Later it was moved across town, completely losing its identity with Old Town. Because of the expense of earthquake refitting, the original building was torn down in 1963.

SMART & FINAL GETS ITS START IN TUSTIN

Smart & Final is a name well known in Tustin, but few know that an early resident founded Santa Ana Wholesale Grocery, which is part of its foundation.

Will C. Crawford and his wife, Effie, came to Tustin City in 1898. They purchased land on Glen Avenue (now Tustin Avenue), south of Main Street, and planted it in walnuts and oranges. They built a family home on the property, and Crawford began accumulating land and establishing a reputation as one of Tustin's leading entrepreneurs.

Other land purchases included fifty acres that he planted with Valencia orange trees in Olive and forty acres devoted to general farming on Newport Avenue in Tustin. Crawford was what they called "a live businessman" in that era and took advantage of what he saw as a great future for Tustin and Orange County.

Crawford joined John Dunstan, Sherm Stevens, C.E. Utt, Victor V. Tubbs, Rufus H. Sanborn and C.J. Cranston in organizing the First National Bank of Tustin in 1911. They took over the building at Main and D, which had been vacated when the Bank of Tustin closed in 1902, and Crawford was selected as president.

His next business venture was to organize the Santa Ana Wholesale Grocery Company in 1912. He became both president and manager of the enterprise and moved the operation into a two-story brick building with a basement that he had built on East First Street near the Santa Fe Railroad station. This was the largest store building in Santa Ana at that time.

Tustin businessman Will C. Crawford organized Santa Ana Wholesale Grocery Company in 1912. After he died, his wife sold it to J.S. Smart, who took a partner named H.D. Final. The business, which is still operating today, then became Smart & Final. Crawford, who came to Tustin in 1898, also was president of the First National Bank of Tustin. *Courtesy of Tustin Area Museum.*

Crawford's success came to a sudden and unexpected halt when he died on November 18, 1912, at the age of fifty. Mrs. Crawford continued to live in their Tustin home and sold the grocery business to J.S. Smart, a banker from Saginaw, Michigan, in 1914. With a partner, H.D. Final, Smart changed the name of the business to Smart & Final and relocated near the docks in San Pedro. By 1919, their sales reached $10 million.

They introduced the cash-and-carry concept in 1923. Until this time even wholesale grocery stores were staffed by clerks who gathered items for the customers. Smart & Final also began locating stores in areas closer to their customers. These two strategies helped them to survive in a highly competitive market.

In 1953, Smart & Final merged with Haas, Baruch, a prominent Los Angeles grocery wholesaler that traced its history back to 1889. The Smart & Final name was retained, although the company moved to Haas, Baruch's new warehouse in Vernon.

The Thriftimart chain acquired the company in 1984. It later closed Thriftimart stores and launched an aggressive modernization and expansion of the Smart & Final units. Today, Smart & Final Corporation has 253 stores in the western United States and northern Mexico.

LOCAL MEN GO OFF TO WAR

Company F, Ninth Infantry, National Guard of California, mustered in Santa Ana in June 1890 with sixty-one men, a captain and two lieutenants.

Although nicknamed "Santa Ana's Own," the company, which was given the designation of Company L shortly after its formation, had at least one Tustin man on its roster. Nelson Miles Holderman, one of seven children in the Upton Holderman family, followed in the footsteps of his father who served in the Civil Was as a member of Company A of the Twenty-second Iowa's Volunteer Infantry. "Neb," as he was known, attended Tustin schools and Occidental College and started his National Guard career as a private and a bugler.

His first service with Company L was in San Francisco after the earthquake and fire in the spring of 1906. Considered a natural tactician, he was deeply interested in military affairs and became a captain when Company L was ordered to Nogales, Arizona, from June to October 1916, during the time of Pancho Villa's raids along the border.

By the time Company L was ordered into the service of the United States on March 26, 1917, Holderman was the commanding officer and the orders from the Adjutant General Boree in Sacramento were sent to Tustin. Other Tustin men joined Company L, as a call went out for eighty-four recruits to bring the company to fighting strength.

After spending several months at Camp Kearny in San Diego County, the Orange County men joined the 40th Division for overseas duty. The company was split up once they arrived in France with its men assigned to various outfits as battle replacements. A number of its members, including Holderman, went to the 307th Infantry, which gained fame as the Lost Battalion.

Surrounded by Germans, six hundred U.S. soldiers with only two days' rations held off the enemy for six days until, through the use of a carrier pigeon, they were discovered and relieved by troops who reached them just in time to save the approximately one hundred men still alive. Captain Holderman was wounded ten times during these six days, but he recovered and served in the Army of Occupation before returning home in the fall of 1919. He earned the Distinguished Service Cross, the Medal of Honor and two Croix de Guerre medals.

Although no other serviceman received the homage of Captain Holderman, some 1,614 Orange County men served during World War I, either overseas or stateside. A total of 55 gave their lives. A gala parade headed by the Home Guards of Orange and Placentia greeted the returnees as they stepped off the train in Santa Ana. All veterans were later honored at a gathering in Irvine Park where medal recipients were recognized.

Most of the approximately fifty Tustin men who had served returned to live in the area. Among those becoming familiar over the years as leaders were Water Bennett, Ives Brown, Grover Fultz, Bill Leinberger, Charles Logan, William Martin, Clarence Pollard, Grover and Lewis Riehl, Ross Schafter, Eddie Squires and Floyd and Forrest Turner.

Louis Riehl, a cavalryman, was among the approximately fifty Tustin men who served in World War I. Many were in Company L under the command of Nelson Miles Holderman, also from Tustin, which became part of the 307th Infantry that gained fame as the Lost Battalion. *Courtesy of Tustin Area Museum.*

CAPTAIN HOLDERMAN RECEIVES MEDAL OF HONOR

Captain Nelson Miles Holderman, a Tustin native who was one of the most decorated U.S. soldiers in World War I, received the Medal of Honor, Distinguished Service Cross and two Croix de Guerre medals. Over thirty thousand people attended ceremonies where he and other Orange County heroes were recognized. *Courtesy of Tustin Area Museum.*

Nelson Miles Holderman, a Tustin native, was considered by many to be one of the most decorated U.S. servicemen in World War I.

His parents, Upton C. and Myra Holderman, natives of Johnson County, Iowa, came to Tustin in 1893 after spending twenty years in Nebraska. They bought twenty acres near Tustin High School's present location and planted oranges, walnuts and apricots. Before too long they added ten more acres of walnuts nearby.

The Holdermans had three daughters, Uppie, Emma and Lyda, and a son, Myron, when they came to Tustin. A second son was born on November 10, 1885, and named Nelson Miles Holderman after Nelson Appleton Miles, a Civil War hero and Medal of Honor recipient. Myron, Nelson and Grant, who was born after Nelson, all attended Tustin Grammar School while John J. Zielian was principal, thus qualifying for membership in Zeke's Bunch.

Holderman began his military career as a private in Santa Ana's National Guard Unit, Company L. He served from June to October 1916 on the Mexican border during the time of Pancho Villas's raids.

In October 1918, Company L was called into active service and sent to France under the command of Holderman, now a captain. The company was assigned as a replacement to Company K, 307th Infantry Regiment, 77th division. They became involved in the fierce battles in the Argonne Forest and earned the name the Lost Battalion after being cut off and surrounded by the enemy for five days.

Official descriptions of the battle noted Captain Holderman as being wounded on October 4, 5 and 7, but throughout the entire period, although he suffered great pain and was subjected to fire of every kind, he continued to lead and encourage the officers and men under his command with unflinching courage and distinguished success in a series of counterattacks against a large German force. On October 6, although wounded, he rushed through enemy machine gun and shell fire and carried two wounded men to a place of safety. His and his company's actions have been credited as the primary reason for repeated German attacks failing to capture the position.

Company L returned to Santa Ana with a rousing welcome in April 1919. At a serviceman's recognition celebration attended by thirty thousand on September 9, 1919, Captain Holderman received the Medal of Honor and the Distinguished Service Cross. He also received two Croix de Guerre medals for his courage and bravery in leading his men.

Hollywood has filmed the story of *The Lost Battalion* twice, the first time in 1919. A 2001 version has Adam James playing Captain Holderman and Rick Shroder starring as his commanding officer, Major Whittlesey.

After returning to Tustin, Captain Holderman rejoined the National Guard and was appointed a colonel. The governor of California named him commandant of the Yountville Soldier's Home, Yountville, California, in 1926. Holderman worked tirelessly for the veterans for over twenty-five years, building new dorms and other facilities including a hospital.

Colonel Holderman and his wife, the former Marguerite Talbot, raised four children while living at the Yountville Soldier's Home. He served until his death on September 3, 1953. He was buried at Golden Gate National Cemetery in San Bruno, California.

Veterans Charter American Legion

American Legion Post 227 was chartered in 1929 with almost thirty of Tustin's leading businessmen and ranchers, all veterans of World War I, as members. These men and their wives, Tustin Unit 227 of the American Legion Auxiliary, were an important part of life in Tustin for many years.

Post 227 defined its role as sponsoring and supporting veterans and their families to promote awareness of the role they played in securing the freedoms and liberties that sustain this country. Members and their wives spent many hours visiting patients in local veterans' hospitals. Over the years, Post 227 sponsored numerous youth activities including a Boy Scout troop, youth environmental conferences, essay and oratorical contests, recognition of the outstanding boy and girl graduate at Tustin Grammar School and sending representatives to Boys and Girls State in Sacramento.

Post 227 continues to sponsor the participation of a young man from each of Tustin's high schools in the California American Legion Boys State. This leadership action program sends qualified high school juniors to Sacramento where they can develop a working knowledge of the structure of government. The Legionnaires also support the American Legion National High School Oratorical contest, a program to develop a better understanding and appreciation of the Constitution, and still recognize outstanding middle school graduates.

The War Memorial Building at First and Prospect was built by Tustin American Legion Post 227 and dedicated to the memory of men who gave their lives in World War II and the Korean conflict. The Legion has been an important part of Tustin since the post was chartered in 1929, sponsoring youth activities in addition to supporting veterans. *Courtesy of Tustin Area Museum.*

After meeting in the Knights of Pythias building for many years, the men and women of Post 227 gathered enough money to construct their own building at the corner of First and Prospect. Known as the War Memorial building, it is dedicated to the memory of Tustin men who gave their lives in defense of their country in World War II and the Korean conflict, including Charles O. Alstot, Edward R. Bristow, John R. Bruns, Edward R. Burrier, Gudalupe Castenada, Ernest R. Costello, Arthur E. Dishman, Marvin E. Gray, Paul C. Kimball Jr., Charles E. Mueller, Ralph P. Pumb, Theodore Taulbee, Derrel C. Wollert, Donald E. Ynigues and Luther D. Yapp.

A second memorial, the Freedom Tree, was added in 1973 in recognition of the POW/MIAs of California. A third plaque dedicated to the City of Tustin, honoring all veterans, was donated by the Veterans of Foreign Wars Post No. 9203, which formed in 1947 but is now inactive.

Post 227 suspended activities for a few years, but it was reactivated in 2002 and now meets in the Tustin Unified School District boardroom. They participate annually in Memorial Day projects and conduct a flag disposal ceremony each year in addition to providing color guards for many meetings and events.

Harry Pieper Opens Feed Store

It is hard to believe today that the area around the intersection of Main and D (El Camino Real) once provided one-stop shopping to the residents of Tustin and outlying areas. A farmer could drive into town, park his truck, do his banking at the First National Bank of Tustin, buy groceries at one of the several markets, pick up needed materials such as pipe or nails at Tustin Hardware, have coffee at the Tustin Drug Store fountain and load up a few bales of alfalfa for his animals, along with a couple of sacks of chicken feed, a few packets of seeds and some seedlings at Piepers Feed Store.

Known as Harry, John F. Pieper opened the feed store in 1918 in a one-story building facing D on the north end of the First National Bank of Tustin, about where Kelly's gift shop is today. Pieper came to Tustin in 1910 from Cincinnati, Ohio, with his fiancée, Norma, and her parents, Fred and Jennie Beckman.

He and Norma were married in February 1915 at a ceremony conducted by the Reverend McDougall of Tustin Presbyterian Church at the Beckman's home. After a honeymoon in San Francisco, they set up housekeeping in a small white house on C Street and continued to work at H. Romer & Company, a general store on Main Street owned by Henry Romer, Norma's uncle. Harry was general manager, and Norma kept the books. A daughter, Audrey, was born in May 1916.

In 1918, the couple rented the one-story building attached to the bank and opened Pieper's Feed Store. Audrey Pieper Forney remembers that she and her brother, Don, who was born in 1923, thought it was a neat place to play with sacks of chicken feed to scramble over and bales of hay and alfalfa to climb. There were also bins of dog biscuits, sunflower seeds, rabbit pellets, salt licks, fertilizers and insecticides, vegetable and flower seeds, trays of seedlings ready for planting—everything for the rural area Tustin was at that time. And there were always lots of cats and kittens.

Pieper had a truck scale constructed beneath the surface of the alley that ran north and south behind the store. One of the few licensed scales in the county, it was used by the Orange County Highway Patrol to weigh possibly

Owner John F. "Harry" Pieper chats with Quincy Page in Pieper's Feed Store during the store's early years. The store opened in 1918 in a building on the north side of the First National Bank of Tustin. A truck scale behind the building was used by the Orange County Highway Patrol to check for overloaded trucks and trailers. *Courtesy of Tustin Area Museum.*

overloaded trucks and trailers. Pieper was called out at all hours of the night and charged fifty cents for opening the scale, as Audrey recalls.

The family moved into a larger home on D Street just south of First shortly after Audrey was born. In addition to running the store, with Norma in charge of bookkeeping, Harry was active in groups working for the betterment of Tustin. He served on the city council for eight years, 1932 to 1940. Don, his son, and David, Audrey's husband, eventually joined him in working in the store.

Norma continued to operate the store after Harry died from a coronary in 1946. Don, David and Don, Audrey and Dave's son, worked with her, along with family friends. Great Western acquired their building when they purchased the First National Bank of Tustin in 1959 and moved that operation into new quarters at the corner of Third and D. Soon authorities decided the old Victorian building was not earthquake safe, and the structure including Pieper's Feed Store was demolished in 1966, ending an era in Tustin history.

Billiard Hall, Not Pool Hall, in 1916

Tustin's first pool room, or the Tustin Billiard Hall, the more elite name chosen by the proprietor Richard McCarthy, opened for the men in Tustin in 1916.

McCarthy, who was a constable in the Tustin Township at the time, selected one of the oldest buildings in town for his establishment. Located on the southeast corner of Main and D (El Camino Real), the western-style wooden building had first housed Harlan Fairbanks's real estate business, then his drugstore.

In 1920, the building was moved east on the south side of Main to make way for building a group of stores, one of which later became the Tustin Food Market. The entire building is now the Cox Building. McCarthy eventually switched from owning a pool hall to owning a gasoline station in Tustin.

The pool hall continued to occupy the relocated building until McCoy's Sheet Metal Works moved into it about 1928. (The McCoys remained in the building until 2003.) Meanwhile, the pool hall relocated to the east side of D Street, north of Main, leasing space in a neoclassical commercial building that had been built by Mr. and Mrs. Charles Cotant at the same time as the Knights of Pythias Hall in 1925. Both of these buildings occupied acreage that had once been occupied by the C.E. Utt home.

One of the oldest buildings in town became the Tustin Billiard Hall, opened by Richard McCarthy on the southeast corner of D (El Camino Real) and Main in 1916. First used by Harlan Fairbanks's real estate business, then his drugstore, the location became a favorite meeting place for the men of the community. *Courtesy of Tustin Area Museum.*

George Smith, pool hall owner at this time, was well known not only for his establishment but also for his peanut roasting machine. Pool players paid five cents for bags of roasted peanuts to accompany their liquid refreshments while they socialized or participated in games of pool.

Charles Cleary, who bought the building around 1940, took over management of the pool hall. It soon had a more elegant moniker, Sportsman Headquarters, complementing the taxidermy studio that Cleary operated in the second storefront on the site.

When Cleary closed the Sportsman Headquarters in 1965, Lillian and Hayden Williams leased the portion where the pool hall had operated. After redecorating the room and adding a lunch counter, they changed the name of the establishment to the Swinging Door.

Now, many years later, the Swinging Door continues to be a popular site for pool, food, drink and sociability, although some of those who knew it in its early days in Tustin might be shocked by the reviews it receives on the Internet. Described as one big open room with pool tables in the middle and places to kick back along the walls, plus a jukebox, it reportedly appeals to everyone from clean-cut, preppy types to bikers to hip-hoppers, "a dive bar where the female bartenders' uniform is a teeny bikini."

It makes one remember Mrs. David Hewes, who complained back in the late 1800s that she saw patrons entering and leaving Liedecker's Saloon when she was rocking in her chair on her front porch. Her husband solved her problem by buying that property and donating it to the Tustin Presbyterian Church.

WCTU Fights Drink

It was a cold December day in 1873 when the Women's Crusade of seventy women went out to pray and plead for abstinence in Hillsborough, Ohio saloons. Continuing their nonviolent protest against the dangers of alcohol, these housewives held pray-ins in local saloons and demanded that the sale of liquor be stopped. In three months they had driven liquor out of 250 communities and for the first time felt what could be accomplished by standing together.

As a result of their action, the national Woman's Christian Temperance Union (WCTU) formally organized in the fall of 1874 in Cleveland, Ohio. The organization sent invitations to other countries in 1883, asking them to form a global WCTU. Now, more than one hundred years later, the WCTU's white ribbon emblem encircles the globe with its motto, "For God, for home and every land." It has become the largest women's organization in the world.

When the movement reached Tustin, a unit, as the groups were called, was formed. By 1902, approximately forty women had taken the pledge. "I hereby solemnly promise, God helping me, to abstain from all distilled, fermented and malt liquors, including wine, beer and cider, as a beverage, and to employ all proper means to discourage the use of, and traffic in the same." Meeting every other Tuesday afternoon at the homes of members, the group also concerned itself with evangelism, health, motherhood, music and sociability. In addition to the officers, president, vice-president, corresponding secretary, treasurer and recording secretary, the local organization had fifteen superintendents (chairwomen), each with a special function.

Going beyond their emphasis on the evils of drink and their watchwords, "Agitate—Educate—Legislate," the ladies were both civic minded and charitable. Many residents of the Tustin community were remembered with bouquets that members made during Flower Missions and delivered to those who were ill or in need of cheering. Tustin soldiers in both World War I and II were the recipients of hand-knitted garments and "comfort bags" filled by members of the group.

The Volstead Act and the enactment of the Eighteenth Amendment to the Constitution, bringing Prohibition to the United States on October 28, 1919, was good news to the WCTU, but it was no reason for the ladies to quit their work. They continued to be one of the first organizations to promote women's rights. The Tustin women kept a close eye on the legislature in Sacramento and joined the national organization in promoting issues involving women, children and world peace.

Mrs. C.E. Utt was a leader in the Women's Christian Temperance Union, a popular organization for the women of Tustin. Taking the pledge, promising to abstain from liquor and discourage the use of it by others, they did everything they could to prevent the use of drink and existence of saloons and liquor stores in the community. *Courtesy of Tustin Area Museum.*

On December 5, 1933, the nation ratified the Twenty-first Amendment, which repealed the Eighteenth Amendment and restored control of alcohol to the states until the creation of the Federal Alcohol Administration in 1935. Tustin's WCTU ladies once more fought drink and the saloons and liquor stores in Tustin. Mrs. C.E. Utt, so they say, personally measured the distance from the front steps of the Tustin Grammar School to the corner of Second and D Streets (El Camino Real) when a small grocery store opening there applied for a liquor license. She counted every foot to be certain that the distance necessary between a school and an establishment selling alcohol was upheld.

Tustin's WCTU continued to function well into the 1980s, but like many other local women's groups, it faltered as older members passed on with no one interested in replacing them.

Chapter 5

Growth Picks Up in 1920s

First High School Opens in 1922

Columbus Tustin established a grammar school almost as soon as his wife and five children joined him in Tustin City from Petaluma, California, in 1870, but fifty years passed before Tustin had a high school.

When the State of California in 1891 offered counties the option of establishing one or more high schools or forming union high school districts, Orange County chose to form unified districts; however, by 1920 only six areas had accomplished this. Anaheim, Capistrano, Fullerton, Huntington Beach and Santa Ana all had high schools. Graduates from Tustin Grammar School with a yen for further education had to attend Santa Ana High School at Tenth and Main or, after 1911, Santa Ana Polytechnic High School on West Walnut.

An article in the *Tustin News* on May 3, 1929, explained that the sponsors of this law had expected Tustin and the Irvine Ranch to be annexed to Santa Ana. However, C.E. Utt helped form a citizens group to fight for the organization of a Tustin Union High School District. This move combined Tustin, Laguna Beach, El Toro, Trabuco Canyon and San Joaquin Elementary School Districts into one unified district—Tustin Union High School—in the spring of 1921.

Although it was far from being the geographical center of this large area, the board of trustees, formed with representatives from each district, selected Tustin as the site of the new school. In short order, the voters approved a

Tustin's first high school opened in the fall of 1922, with the first graduation on June 8, 1923. The beautiful $350,000 neoclassic building had a one-thousand-seat auditorium, an outdoor Greek theater and gymnasium and swimming pool in addition to the usual classrooms. The original building was declared unsafe in case of earthquakes and razed in 1966. *Courtesy of Tustin Area Museum.*

bond issue of $250,000, and the board purchased fifteen acres on Laguna Road between Newport Avenue and Red Hill. The board paid Clarence Bowman and Jacob Fink $41,000 for the property, which included a house that could be used by the superintendent of schools, and hired Mott M. Marston, a Los Angeles architect, to design the building, which would be constructed by local contractors William Bowman and George Preble.

That fall about seventy-five students attended classes in temporary quarters at the Tustin Primary and Grammar School location. The beautiful, $350,000 neoclassical building with a one-thousand-seat auditorium, an outdoor Greek theater, domestic science department, mechanical and manual training departments, athletic field and gymnasium opened the following year, with the first class graduating in 1923. Three years later, a new wing was added, then a larger gymnasium and a swimming pool.

Although a family sedan was sufficient to bring students to and from Laguna the first year, a complex transportation schedule that allowed students to stay after school for sports and other activities quickly developed. Tustin Union High School was in the transportation business as well as education.

J.W. Means came from Banning, California, to open the school as its first superintendent, and he remained at the helm until his death in 1940. Many of the early teachers, including Emma B. Hield, Stella Yocum, Madge Stephens and Clara Macomber, stayed at Tustin until they retired.

In 1966, the original building was judged unsafe in case of an earthquake. It took wreckers ten days to demolish the structure during July of that year.

The old building was replaced with the current facility, which, without the charm of the original Tustin Union High School, continues to carry on its excellent traditions, succeeding in both sports and academics.

Tustin Union High School District merged with Tustin Elementary School District on July 1, 1972, becoming part of Tustin Unified School District. A California Distinguished School, Tustin High has been recognized by *Newsweek* magazine as one of the top six hundred high schools in the nation.

CITIZENS VOTE TO INCORPORATE

Tustin was a charming, tree-shaded, cohesive little town by mid-1920. Longtime resident Louise Artz Archibald once described it as "a beautiful and adventure-filled neighborhood."

Citrus was king in the outlying areas, with three orange packinghouses offering abundant seasonal employment. Homes ranging from simple bungalows to elaborate Victorians lined the shady streets. Two churches, the First Advent Christian and First Presbyterian, took care of spiritual needs. The downtown area housed a bank and a number of stores, including several grocery stores, a drugstore, feed store and a hardware store. The Knights of Pythias Lodge, with its newly constructed building, and the American Legion met social needs. A primary school, an elementary school and a high school, as well as a library, provided education. A weekly newspaper kept the citizens informed.

Santa Ana's attempt to claim the town by annexation had been rebuffed, although many still worried that they'd try again. Tustin's only negatives, as far as most of its nine hundred residents were concerned, were a lack of police and fire protection, but a group of community leaders disagreed. They urged that the advantages of incorporation were needed, so they collected candidates for a city council and organized an election.

A total of 248 residents responded to their call on September 14, 1927, and passed incorporation with 138 "yes" votes and 110 "no" votes. The newly elected city council included Charles Logan, William Huntley, Edmund Kiser and Fred Schwendeman, with Byron "Barney" Crawford as mayor; Walter J. Pollard, treasurer; and J.R. Harbour, city clerk.

City offices were set up in borrowed space in the Knights of Pythias building, and councilmen went to work. Kiser took charge of streets,

Byron "Barney" Crawford was elected the first mayor of Tustin in 1927 when residents voted to incorporate. He received 136 votes, while incorporation received 138 "yes" votes and "110" no votes from a total of 248 voters. He served as mayor for five years. *Courtesy of Tustin Area Museum.*

walks and parks; Logan became fire and police commissioner; Huntley took over lights and power; and Schwendeman assumed responsibility for health and safety.

John L. Stanton was hired from Huntington Beach to be the first chief of police. He would stay in office until 1942. The existing volunteer fire department continued to serve with its firetruck, a converted 1912 Buick touring car donated by Sam Tustin, kept at Huntley's Tustin Garage.

By 1931, both the volunteer fire department and the city offices had moved into a small, newly built building on Third Street, but there were no full-time firemen until 1962. The Orange County Fire Authority later took over fire service in Tustin. The present Civic Center, with a city hall and headquarters for the police department, was built in 1974.

The day-to-day jobs handled by the original city council are now spread among a city manager, city attorney, city clerk, personnel services, planning commission, community development, finance, parks and recreation and public works departments and a redevelopment agency.

In a recent nationwide survey conducted by *Forbes* magazine, in collaboration with ZoomProspector, a San Francisco consulting firm, Tustin ranked among "America's Top 25 Towns to Live Well." *Money* magazine included Tustin on its list of "Best Places to Retire" in 2005.

FIRST POLICEMAN HIRED

Quiet, little Tustin was a place where everyone felt safe and no one locked their doors. But after it incorporated as a city on September 15, 1927, the newly elected city council felt that, as a city, Tustin should have a police department. In January 1928, they hired John L. Stanton, a Huntington Beach police officer, to form a police department.

Starting with the title street superintendent, Stanton became chief of police after two months, working for forty-five dollars a month. The chief of police had a title but little else. There was no police department building and no police car. The 1910 Craftsman-style house that Stanton and his wife, Kathryn, moved into at 515 West Third Street served as the police station, with their personal telephone doubling as the police department communication system. Stanton's personal car was the official police vehicle while he was on duty.

John L. Stanton, Tustin's first policeman, and city councilman Charlie Logan, who was also the fire and police commissioner, stand by Stanton's personal car that doubled as the city's police vehicle until the city council authorized purchase of a police car. Stanton served as a one-man police force for fourteen years. *Courtesy of Tustin Area Museum.*

Changes came as Stanton continued to be Tustin's one-man police department for the next fourteen years. The city council authorized purchase of a police car. Eventually, space for a police department and city hall was rented on Main Street.

Stanton worked alone until the city approved hiring a night patrolman in 1942. To be sure that Stanton was kept busy, he was also appointed to serve as inspector of buildings, plumbing and electrical installation. There is no record of his salary at that time, but because the new night patrolman was hired at $125 a month, it seems likely that his compensation had been increased.

Stanton continued to do double duty until George Broomell took over as city building inspector. He then became business license collector as well as chief of police. In 1948, the city hired a third officer on a six-month trial basis and later made him permanent.

While on duty, Big John—as he became known due to his six-foot, five-inch frame, usually parked on Main by the side entrance to the drugstore at the intersection of D (El Camino Real) and Main, ready to chase any motorist speeding or failing to stop at the intersection. D Street was part of California State Highway 101 at that time, connecting with Laguna Road and serving as the main route south with heavy traffic, especially on weekends.

Big John became a legend during the war years. Marines from El Toro delighted in trying to outsmart him. A favorite tale, true or not, tells how a couple of guys distracted him while several others secured the rear bumper of his squad car to a tree, then laughed uproariously when he tried to take off after another prankster racing through town at high speed.

While Marines might tease him, local teenagers had a healthy respect for his law and order. One encounter with him was enough. Seldom did he have to get on their case a second time.

Stanton retired as Tustin began to grow after World War II. He probably never dreamed that the tiny police department that he inaugurated would grow to nearly one hundred sworn police officers and fifty-five civilian support personnel or that the City of Tustin would cover approximately 12.3 square miles with a population of over seventy thousand.

Community Develops Traditions

Tustin was a close-knit community with much camaraderie in its early years. The intersection of Main and D (El Camino) was the center of activity. Those living in town and those from the outlying citrus ranches congregated here, creating many traditions.

Each day at midmorning, a bell would sound loud and clear. Wielded by the druggist or a Tustin Drug Store employee, the clanging instrument announced to all within hearing distance that coffee was ready. Businessmen and any ranchers in town for shopping or banking would crowd into the store, hustling to get a stool at the counter and claim their mug of coffee.

The news of the day, both local and national, as well as the latest stories and jokes, passed up and down the counter, along with the sugar and cream. These exchanges would reach the entire community by nightfall.

Ranchers might miss coffee, but they never failed to stop at Tustin Hardware before returning home. This store (now Mrs. B's) next to the First National Bank was a refuge for Tustin men during its eighty-seven years of existence and more than a half dozen owners.

Men, usually from outside town, could be found relaxing and enjoying the companionship of their friends in a circle of battered chairs and benches pulled up to a pot-bellied wood stove in the back of the store. In addition to learning the latest news, they could count on finding in stock any tool or product they needed.

The clientele had changed to homeowners, apartment managers, repairmen and the like, and the wood stove had been removed by the time the store closed in 1997, but men still knew they could find whatever they needed, including friendship and conversation.

The third place the men considered their own in Tustin was down the street at the corner of C and Main. The Horseshoe Club met here for nearly fifty years. Originally the site of Marlow's Blacksmith Shop, the tree-shaded lot was a haven for businessmen and ranchers who liked a game of horseshoes.

Children walking home from Tustin Grammar School often lingered to watch as a player assumed his pitching pose and propelled a horseshoe toward the target, a metal stake, with a loud clang signaling a ringer. Smoking and shooting the breeze occupied other men lounging on the shady benches.

A circle of chairs pulled up to the pot-bellied stove at the rear of Tustin Hardware was a favorite meeting place for Tustin men. They also found companionship and conversation at the bar of the local billiard parlor, morning coffee time at the Tustin Drug Store soda fountain and the horseshoe pits at the corner of Main and C. *Courtesy of Tustin Area Museum.*

When Larry Fricker needed more space for his fertilizer-and-agricultural-supply business, the club moved to a shady location on Main, east of D. The property, part of an orange grove owned by the John Prescott family, was used until 1962 when Saddleback Chapel was built.

Tustin Billiard Parlor, later known as Tustin Pool Room, then Sportsman Headquarters, was a haven for men for many years, although as the Swinging Door, it now has women among its patrons. Located originally on Main Street, east of D, it moved to its present location in the mid-1920s, with George Smith as owner. A peanut machine that roasted nuts to perfection was added at that time, with the goobers selling for five cents a bag.

Charley Cleary bought the establishment in 1940 and operated it in conjunction with his taxidermy shop. Hayden and Lillian Williams took over in 1965 and added the lunch counter, which is still popular today.

TUSTIN NEWS PRINTS PREMIERE EDITION

Amazingly, the *Tustin News* was preceded by four other weekly publications, none of which lasted longer than one issue.

Dates are foggy, but there's evidence, according to author-historian Jim Sleeper, that a paper called the *Telegraph* printed its first and only issue prior to 1900. Another publication, entitled *Tustin Sentinel*, made a brief appearance shortly after that. Then there was a lull until the *Enterprise* appeared in 1911, followed by William Perry's *Tustin News* in 1914.

Eight years later, in November 1922, a tramp printer from Beaver City, Utah, Timothy Brownhill, printed the first edition of the *Tustin News*, using equipment that he had shipped from Utah. Brownhill operated a print shop in downtown Tustin in conjunction with publishing a weekly paper that covered local events.

Warmly welcomed by Santa Ana's *Daily Register*, the new publisher praised Tustin's residents and businessmen for their support, but despite his supposedly glowing success, he soon sold out to the Reverend John Winterbourne and his sons, Frank and Dale. They transferred their interest to F.H. Fowler in 1925, and he continued as publisher for ten years.

Clyde and Gretchen Simmons, the next owners, also kept the paper for ten years. But from 1945 until 1956, when William A. Moses II and his wife, Lucille, bought the publication, the *Tustin News* had five different owners. William Mast, who bought it from the Simmons, resold it to Ed Reed and George Bronzan in less than a year. They sold the weekly to Harry Young the next year, and he published it for a year before selling to James Quinn. After about eight years, Quinn sold to Bob and Peg Evans, who continued for a year before selling to Moses.

Moses, a Stanford graduate, was an experienced newspaper man with service as a war correspondent, a reporter at the *Bakersfield Californian*, a religion editor at the *Los Angeles Times* and editor of the *Newport Harbor News Press*. He always claimed that he bought the *Tustin News* as well as a home in the Tustin area because he wanted to be able to go home for lunch, but it soon became apparent that both he and his wife wanted to become an essential part of a small community.

Moses devoted almost forty years of effort to projects bettering Tustin, helping to form a chamber of commerce, assisting in establishing the Tustin Area Woman's Club, working to achieve an annexation that cut off Santa

Bill Moses, *right*, who published the *Tustin News* for almost forty years, is shown with his young son, William A. Moses III, and his father, William Chauncey Moses. Moses was responsible for organizing the first Tiller Day celebration, helping to revive the chamber of commerce and encouraging formation of the Tustin Area Woman's Club. *Courtesy of Tustin Area Museum.*

Ana, helping to gain an off ramp from the 5 Freeway at Newport Avenue and the victorious vote for sewer bonds on the third try. He was the spark behind the first Tiller Days celebration and was named 1958 Tustin Area Man of the Year.

Lucille raised a son, William A. Moses III, better known as Scooper, and a daughter, Penny, in addition to writing poetry and a column for the *Tustin News.* She was active in the Tustin Area Woman's Club, Jack and Jill Guild and Assistance League of Tustin, as well as other women's organizations.

Moses sold to the *Orange County Register* in 1995. Both he and Lucille have passed on, but their son is a Tustin businessman.

Local Runner Wins Olympic Gold Medal

The community was ecstatic when a young Tustin woman won a gold medal in the four-hundred-meter relay as a member of the United States women's relay team at the 1932 Olympics in the Los Angeles Coliseum.

As a child, Evelyn Furtsch was known for winning any race she entered. At Tustin High School, there was no girls' track, so she played basketball, field hockey and baseball. Her gym teacher, Grace Shults, told the Tustin track coach, Vincent Humeston, how fast she was, so he invited her to run with the boys' track team and was impressed enough to contact the Los Angeles Athletic Club about training for the coming Olympics in 1932.

Aileen Allen, who was training a few girls, invited her to try out with them. Evelyn won all the races and was asked to join the group. When the Los Angeles Athletic Club sent three girls to a national meet in New Jersey in 1931, Evelyn was one of them. After an eleven-day car trip across the country with Humeston and her mother, Evelyn came in second at the meet, beating Stella Walsh, who was considered a world champion, and won a silver medal in the one hundred meters.

Encouraged by this, Evelyn decided to train for the 1932 Olympics with Humeston as her coach. When Olympic tryouts were held in Chicago in 1932 in the midst of the Depression, the Los Angeles Athletic Club couldn't afford to send the girls they had been training; however, the Tustin Chamber of Commerce came to Evelyn's rescue, going door to door to raise money to send her, her mother and Humeston to Chicago. They collected $190, and the trio drove to Chicago in Humeston's car and stayed with Mrs. Furtsch's cousin.

Evelyn won her preliminary heat and her semifinal heat but fell at the tape in the finals. She was disqualified and eliminated from the Olympic team, but when Humeston called Aileen Allen to explain what had happened, he was instructed to bring her home quickly. A message that she was going to be on the team was waiting when they arrived in Tustin.

Evelyn joined six other girls in Los Angeles and began training with Olympic coach George Vreeland. When he selected the relay team, it included Mary Carew as first runner; Evelyn, second; Annette Rogers, third; and Wilhelmina von Bremen, fourth. The relay was one of the last events in the Olympics, so the girls had a week to practice passing the baton and polish their teamwork.

After breaking both the Olympic and the world record, running the relay in 46.9 seconds, the runners received gold medals, which were packaged in boxes and not attached to ribbons as they are today, but the ceremony with the American flag being raised and the national anthem played was the same awe-inspiring event as athletes experience today.

Evelyn returned home to a flurry of recognition ceremonies and banquets. She enrolled at Santa Ana College in the fall. By the time the next Olympics

Evelyn Furtsch, *center*, a student at Tustin High School, always loved to run whether for fun at the beach or on the track. Encouraged by track coach Vincent Humeston, she trained for the 1932 Olympics in Los Angeles and earned a place on the women's relay team that won a gold medal in the four-hundred-meter relay. *Courtesy of Tustin Area Museum.*

were held, she was married to Joe Ojeda and had a baby daughter. She later had a son and eventually became a Realtor. She is still a Tustin resident.

As she says, "When we ran in 1932 we just loved to run and loved to be a part of something as exciting as the Olympics. It was only part of our life and when it was over, we went back to doing our own thing."

Population Rattles and Rolls in 1933 Earthquake

March 10, 1933, 5:54 p.m.: Tustin, along with the rest of Orange County, reeled in the Long Beach earthquake.

That evening is stamped indelibly into my memory. My parents and I were seated at the heavy, old table in the kitchen, eating the last bites of our supper. Mother had brought to the table a banana cream pie that she had baked that afternoon and was cutting wedges for our dessert.

Suddenly a noise—one I could never describe until I heard a sonic boom—shattered the quiet. The table heaved and bucked like a small boat in stormy seas. We tried to rise, but the tilt of the table threw us back into our chairs. Weird noises, pounding, rattling, creaking and groaning, added to our confusion and fear.

When the table finally stilled, we struggled to our feet and rushed to the back door. There we were stopped by a cascade of bricks blocking the screen door. Mother and I huddled behind my dad until no more bricks rolled off the roof. Then he forced the door open, and we stumbled over piles of bricks on the porch and steps as we exited into the back yard.

The giant walnut tree was still swaying and bending, its branches sweeping the ground. Except for the rustle of the tree, the evening was eerily quiet. No birds called, no dogs barked.

There was no such thing as disaster training in those days. We went back into the house and started calling the family to be sure they were safe. Amazingly, the telephone operator was still on duty. My aunt in Orange reported being scared but without damage. Relatives in Santa Ana also had been spared, but fearing another quake, they were hesitant to remain in their house and soon arrived to camp in our back yard until they felt it was safe to return home.

Tustin Grammar School was the only building in Tustin to sustain major damage in the 1933 earthquake. Repairs, which included removing the second floor auditorium and replacing brick facing, took almost a year. Classes were held in empty store buildings and the First Presbyterian Church Sunday School rooms during this time. *Courtesy of Tustin Area Museum.*

Rumors flew as aftershocks continued. Several people pulled into our drive to warn us that if the Irvine Dam broke, the area would be flooded. Others came to report hundreds injured and hurt in Santa Ana, Anaheim and Long Beach.

The next day, despite aftershocks, was sightseeing day. People swarmed into downtown Santa Ana, gaping at the damage while police, the National Guard and volunteers from the American Legion watched for looters and tried to maintain order. I still remember seeing a hotel with one side missing. The open rooms with beds and dressers still in place reminded me of a dollhouse.

Tustin Grammar School was the only building in Tustin with major damage. The school lost its brick face and second-floor auditorium. Classes met in vacant store buildings and the Tustin Presbyterian Church for almost a year while repairs were made. The First National Bank lost some trim and later removed its turrets as a precaution. Many homes suffered a few cracks in their ceilings or plaster walls, but only Los Alisos, the Roy Ozmun house where Madame Modjeska once lived, had extensive damage; however, some fifty homes reported that their chimneys needed repair or replacement.

Auto Camp Built to Serve Travelers

Auto camps and auto courts came into being in the late 1920s and 1930s, as the automobile became common and family vacations began to center around driving. Because these vacationers either didn't want to stop at hotels or couldn't afford to do so, campgrounds and small cottages offering sleeping, cooking and bathroom facilities, as well as a garage for the family auto, began to appear along the highways.

Basil F.H. Brewster brought his wife, Grace, and two sons, Basil and Fred, to Tustin from New York State in 1937 with the idea of buying land and building an auto court. He settled on a piece of property in the heart of Tustin at the corner of Main and D (El Camino Real) Streets. A Gilmore gasoline station took a chunk out of the parcel at the corner, leaving it shaped like an upside-down L, with the long portion fronting D Street and the leg ending on Main next to store building that was then housing the Tustin Library.

As Basil—who still lives in the area—remembers, his dad had no previous experience as a carpenter, but he sketched plans for four cottages to be built in a unit running east and west on the south side of the property and built

Brewster's Auto Camp was a welcome stop for weary motorists. Basil F.H. Brewster built the motel on a piece of property in the heart of Tustin at the corner of Main and D (El Camino Real). The family lived in one unit, and the rest were rented out to travelers or visitors to the El Toro Marine Base. *Courtesy of Tustin Area Museum.*

it himself, hiring unemployed men who came to the site seeking work as helpers. Basil recalls helping to shingle the roof. When the cottages were finished, the family moved into the one at the front and began renting the other three to travelers. Work began the next year on a second unit on the north side of the property, parallel to the first.

Lumber for this addition was purchased from Barr Lumber in Santa Ana, as Basil recalls, and one of their employees drew up the plans. When work was completed, the Brewsters had seven units to manage. The war cut into the number of travelers on the road, but Basil remembers people who worked at the El Toro Marine Base staying long term, as well as others like a high-ranking naval officer who traveled regularly to San Diego and stopped in Tustin.

Anticipating the changes that would come after the war, Brewster sold the motel and bought a home on San Juan Street. A 1945 directory lists the auto court as the Tustin Motel, with W.G. Olson as owner. The buildings eventually were remodeled into an office complex that still exists between the Vintage Lady and the Roach Building.

Another Tustin auto court was located on Second Street. The units ran down Second toward Prospect from the corner of D, behind a small eating place originally called the Auto Court Cafe. This counter-and-stool cafe changed names frequently: Marian's Cafe, Jewett's Auto Court and Trucker's Inn appeared on the sign before it became Ruby's in the mid-1940s, although the auto court continued to be known as Jewett's. The cafe closed in 1982, and the building, including the auto court, was torn down in 1990. The property is now a parking lot for Helm Chiropractic, Inc., owned by Dr. Robert Helm.

A Filling Station on Every Corner

Years ago, motorists were not concerned with the miles per gallon or the fuel economy offered by the cars they drove. Gasoline was plentiful and cheap, and cars were gas guzzlers by today's standards. As my dad once commented when he was test driving a new Dodge sedan, "This car can pass anything but a service station."

Tustin met the demand with almost a dozen filling stations, as they were called then, and garages with gasoline pumps on the less than two-mile strip of Highway 101 passing through the community. Motorists approaching Tustin from the west on First Street negotiated a broad curve into D Street (El Camino Real), passed through the heart of the downtown area, then made another curve onto Laguna Road just past Sixth Street, crossed Newport Avenue and passed in front of Tustin High School as they headed to Irvine, El Toro, Laguna Canyon Road, San Juan Capistrano, San Clemente, Oceanside and San Diego.

Park's Texaco at First and Tustin Avenue greeted them as they approached the outskirts of Tustin. Two more blocks and Case's Smiling Associated station and Jerome Kidd's automotive repair were ready to serve them at Mountain View and First. Three blocks east at C Street, Becker's Garage advertised Fords and Mercurys, in addition to repairs, tires, batteries and accessories.

Bristow's Signal anchored the southeast side of the curve onto D Street from First, and three blocks south at Third Street Carson and Golding offered tire recapping, tires, lubes, batteries and Shell gasoline. A Gilmore station proclaimed "Roar with Gilmore" at Main and D. Just around the corner, between D and C on the north side of Main, Oscar A. Leihy, who started with a bicycle repair shop and sporting goods store, had added an automotive garage to his business mix. Tustin Garage did repairs and pumped gas at Sixth Street. If a motorist failed to stop at one of these suppliers, he had a last chance at either a Chevron or Signal station as he left town.

Oscar Leihy originally owned a bicycle repair shop and a sporting goods store in Tustin. He began to repair automobiles as they became popular, and when traffic increased through Tustin, he added a garage and gasoline pumps to the location on Main Street in of the center of town. *Courtesy of Tustin Area Museum.*

Amazingly, all these stations and garages stayed in business for years, although the owners frequently changed. Bristow's Signal became Tustin Service when Kenneth Cawthon bought it in the early '30s and switched to Mobil Oil. Harry Holmes bought the station some ten years later but kept the Tustin Service name. Console & Sisson bought out Becker. Later, Kidd moved his business into the building. The Gilmore station became Daniel's Mobil. The Signal station was originally owned by L.L. Hood, but Austin Pierson took over in the late '40s, and Frank Greinke later occupied the premises. Tustin Garage was started by William Huntley and Nick Gulick in 1915 and survived into the current century, although the owners changed several times. Most recently, the building was refurbished as Beach Pit BBQ.

Early service stations operated differently than today's self-service operations. The high school boys hired to serve customers not only filled the tank, they checked the oil level, added water to the radiator, put air in the tires and washed all the windows. In addition, a motorist could often get a map or at least directions to guide them on the highway.

Chapter 6

World War II Changes Tustin Forever

Pearl Harbor Attack Stuns Community

Sunday, December 7, 1941: breakfast was over, the dishes were washed, many families had departed for church, others were settling in with the Sunday paper and kids were arguing over the funny pages while their parents were wishing they would go outside and leave them in peace.

Then a message interrupting a program on the radio or a voice at the other end of the ringing telephone shattered the tranquility: "The Japanese have bombed Pearl Harbor." The rest of the day was spent huddled in front of the radio, waiting for news flashes. Anger grew as newscasters reported eight battleships attacked with five sunk, including the USS *Arizona*, three light cruisers, three destroyers, three small vessels damaged and 188 aircraft destroyed plus casualties, including 1,104 men on the USS *Arizona*.

A war extra printed by the *Santa Ana Register* on December 8 called the action an "unprovoked and dastardly attack" and reported that Congress had declared war after being addressed by President Roosevelt. His message, which was broadcast to the nation, declared December 7 "a day which will live in infamy." On December 11, the United States joined Great Britain and declared war on Germany and Italy.

Tustin was not completely unprepared for war. American Legion Post 227 had set up a California Air Warning System Post the month before to identify aircraft and report the findings to the West Los Angeles Filter Center of the Fourth Fighter Command. Ruth Cox and Grace Leinberger, who had traveled to Pasadena to train as instructors, were teaching volunteers who would work in pairs on eight-hour shifts, providing twenty-four-hour coverage. Men were assigned to night shifts, while women worked during the day at a small tower in an Irvine bean field. In addition, a listening post had been established on Newport Avenue north of Seventeenth Street.

After December 7, the Tustin Volunteer Fire Department promptly divided Tustin into ten sections and appointed teams to patrol each one. These air raid wardens enforced blackout rules. Residents put up blackout curtains to keep light from showing from their homes, and motorists covered their headlights with tape to allow only small slits of light. A Police and Fire Bulletin No. 1 issued on December 12 outlined blackout rules and the signal—two blasts of the fire siren at thirty-second intervals—to be used for air raid warnings.

Tustin citizens eased their anger over the Japanese bombing of Pearl Harbor in many ways, including the purchase of war bonds. Children at Tustin Elementary School joined the effort, filling books with saving stamps and redeeming them for war bonds to purchase a jeep. Here the student body celebrates at a bond rally with army officials. *Courtesy of Tustin Area Museum.*

Incensed by what the Japanese had done, the young men, and some not so young, promptly enlisted. On the home front, Tustin citizens counteracted their anger and fear by signing up for ration books, buying war bonds, planting victory gardens and canning the fruits and vegetables they grew. The Reverend Calvin Duncan of the Tustin Presbyterian Church started a newsletter for servicemen. When he was assigned to another church, Winifred Humeston took over, and by the end of the war in 1944, 450 copies of *With the Boys in Service* were being mailed every month.

World War II changed Tustin forever. Personnel from the Santa Ana Army Air Base, the U.S. Navy lighter-than-air base and the USMC Station at El Toro discovered that the small town with a population of less than one thousand was a charming place to live. Many returned after the war, and the village began to grow. Now, Tustin is a thriving area occupying over eleven square miles with a population near seventy thousand people.

Japanese Farmers Relocated to Arizona

The forest of transmission towers at the electrical substation on the northeast corner of Bryan and Browning gives little indication of what once occupied that space.

During the 1920s, 1930s and early years of 1940, this corner was home to a small Japanese settlement of approximately thirty-five families who leased land from the Irvine Company to grow vegetable crops such as celery and tomatoes. Their farms were on Irvine land abutting Tustin, as well as in nearby canyons including Peters Canyon and Rattlesnake Canyon. The Irvine Company allowed the Japanese, who were prevented by law from owning land, to lease farms but prohibited them from living on the land.

Children from families living in the Bryan/Browning community attended Tustin schools. Families living farther out on the Irvine Ranch sent their children to Irvine Grammar School. Everyone came by bus to Tustin High, and many continued their education at Santa Ana Junior College.

Although there was little socializing outside of the classroom, these young people were an intricate part of our school lives. They ranked among the brightest and most athletic. They participated in clubs and student government and made their letters in sports.

The Bryan/Browning settlement was the center of activity for all Japanese families living on the Irvine Ranch because it had a large wooden hall that was used for the Irvine Japanese Language School, called Gakuto. Founded in 1929, this school held Japanese classes for the young people on Saturdays in addition to offering evening classes for adults.

The hall that faced Bryan Avenue also was used for meetings of the Young Women's Association and the Young Men's Association. These groups held annual events such as a Mother's Day Tea, a Father's Day celebration and a Sports Day.

The nearest Buddhist temple at that time was in Los Angeles. Most Irvine families made the trip to attend it only on special occasions. Children from at least one family came into downtown Tustin to attend Tustin Presbyterian Church Sunday school.

The small wooden houses were basic—primitive by today's standards. Windmills provided energy to pump water from a well on the property and generate some electricity, but many homes used oil lamps. Indoor plumbing was limited to a water faucet.

Because Tustin was the nearest town, many families patronized the Tustin Hardware store, First National Bank and the downtown grocery stores.

Japanese farmers cultivated land leased from the Irvine Company, growing celery, tomatoes and other vegetables from the 1920s until World War II, when they were banished from the area to a relocation camp in Arizona. *Courtesy of Tustin Area Museum.*

Small trucks known as shopping wagons came from Los Angeles with special provisions such as tofu and rice.

The settlement was abandoned when the families were forced to leave the area after the start of World War II. A few former residents eventually returned to Orange County, but the small Japanese community never reformed.

Residents Join War Effort

"The Japanese have bombed Pearl Harbor!" That message shocked the nation long ago on Sunday morning, December 7, 1941, but few, if any, Tustin residents have forgotten where they were and what they were doing when they heard the news.

Gushing from the radio and passing from person to person, the news was terrifying. What would happen next? Would Japanese war planes swoop down on Long Beach where U.S. Navy ships were anchored or Los Angeles or even Tustin? We prayed that nothing would happen and stayed glued to the radio for as long as we could stay awake. By morning, our terror had lessened somewhat.

Despite headlines, news broadcasts and President Roosevelt's proclamation of war, the daily routine continued almost normally for a short time. Then blackouts with blackout curtains, curfews and limited night driving with headlights taped to allow only a small slit of light to pass through became normal. Volunteering as air raid wardens and air craft spotters, along with air raid siren tests and rationing of gas, meat, sugar and shoes, became accepted parts of our lives.

Many senior boys left Tustin High before graduation, volunteering for the army or navy. Japanese students vanished overnight, banished with their parents to relocation camps. Women and kids were suddenly in demand to replace workers who had been drafted. Summer vacation was extended into October so that students could continue to work in the fields during harvest.

We gradually became less fearful, although Tustin was surrounded by the navy lighter-than-air base, El Toro Marine Base and the army air base at Costa Mesa. The majority of traffic to and from El Toro traveled through Tustin on D Street (El Camino Real). Residents were both terrified and fascinated by long caravans of equipment and military personnel passing through at all hours.

Volunteer aircraft spotters from Tustin were assigned to an aircraft-listening post in Irvine during World War II. Gertrude Cleary was one of the many women serving. Volunteering as air raid wardens and coping with blackouts, air raid siren tests and the rationing of gas, meat, sugar and shoes became accepted parts of our lives. *Courtesy of Tustin Area Museum.*

Several times we thought the community was under attack, but fortunately, all episodes were false alarms. The scariest happening came one night shortly after everyone was in bed. The air raid siren atop the First National Bank building howled. The night was pitch-black. Long fingers of light suddenly illuminated the western sky behind Santa Ana. We watched for what seemed like hours before the search lights flickered out and the air raid siren signaled "all clear."

The next day—and for years after—there were whispered accounts of an enemy plane shot down over Long Beach or a submarine sunk while it was trying to penetrate the entrance to Los Angeles Harbor. But to this day, no one seems to know what really happened.

We had frequent air raid drills at school, but one day the situation seemed completely different. While the siren blasted, the teachers quickly lined us up against the lockers in the downstairs hall. We sat on the floor for a least an hour, telling jokes, giggling and trying to act nonchalant and hide our terror. The all-clear signal finally sounded without incident, but we never learned why the drill lasted so long.

The war ended with Tustin unscathed, but everything had changed. The community would never again be a sleepy, small town.

Lighter-Than-Air Base Replaces Bean Field

World War II is long past, but Tustin still has two majestic airship hangers as reminders of the role our town played during the hostilities.

Although most local residents referred to it as the navy lighter-than-air (LTA) base, Santa Ana Naval Air Station was the official name of the base established and commissioned here in September 1942. Occupying 1,383 acres of agricultural land acquired from Irvine, the station supported observation blimps and personnel necessary to conduct antisubmarine patrols off the Southern California coast during World War II.

After the attack on Pearl Harbor in 1941, the navy asked Congress for authorization to purchase an increased number of airships. By June 1942, Congress had authorized the construction of 200 airships. During the war, Goodyear built a total of 168. At peak production, the company was turning out 11 airships a month.

Six of these airships could fit into each of the two hangars constructed in Tustin. Labeled the world's largest unsupported, timber-constructed buildings, the massive structures were built at a cost of $2.5 million each. Both are 1,088 feet long, 178 feet high and 297 feet wide. This translates to being as high as an eighteen-story building and as long as three football fields. The doors are composed of six leaves, each weighing twenty-six to twenty-nine tons. The hangars were designated as National Historical Landmarks in August 1978.

The facility served as an LTA base until it was decommissioned in June 1949. During the Korean conflict, the station was reactivated in May 1951 and commissioned as Marine Corps Air Facility Santa Ana. The name was changed to Marine Corps Air Station (Helicopter) Santa Ana in September 1969 and finally MCAS Tustin in June 1985. It was the country's first air facility developed solely for helicopter operations. The name Santa Ana was originally attached to the base because it was located in an unincorporated area.

Identified as the world's largest, unsupported timber-constructed buildings, two massive structures were built at a cost of $2.5 million each at the naval lighter-than-air base. Each hangar was as high as an eighteen-story building and as long as three football fields. A half dozen World War II blimps could fit inside each one. *Courtesy of Tustin Area Museum.*

MCAS Tustin closed in July 1999. Approximately 1,294 acres have been conveyed to the City of Tustin, private developers and public institutions for a combination of residential, commercial, educational and public recreational and open-space uses. The City of Tustin is developing Tustin Legacy (residential) and the District (commercial) on the property. South Orange County Community College District, Rancho Santiago Community College District, Advanced Technology Education Park, Orange County Sheriff Department training facility and the Orange County Rescue Mission are other occupants.

The Northern Hangar, located near Valencia Avenue and Armstrong Road, is currently proposed to be ultimately conveyed by the Department of the Navy to the County of Orange. The current Tustin Legacy Reuse Plan and Specific Plan show the 11-acre hangar facility, located on an 84.5-acre parcel, identified as a County of Orange Regional Park.

The South Hangar will be ultimately conveyed to Tustin Legacy Community Partners, LLC, the master developer of 820 acres at Tustin

Legacy. When they choose to redevelop the hangar site, they will be required to comply with the MCAS Tustin Specific Plan, which identifies a variety of possible uses. At present, the hangar is used for shooting movies and TV programs.

Many suggestions have been made for the hangar's future use, but current maps designate it as "GO," meaning it will be torn down.

Summer Theater Scores Hit

Residents of Tustin have long appreciated drama and music, starting in the late 1800s when they applauded traveling shows at Santa Ana's Opera House or reveled in theatrical and musical soirees featuring entertainment by hostesses such as Coralinn Rice, Madame Modjeska and Stella Preble Nau.

Unfortunately, the town hit a creative dry spell after the turn of the century. Those longing for dramatic entertainment had only the plays put on by the drama students at Tustin High School. Then things changed in the late 1940s.

It was a summer day at the beach when Florence and Harold Turney of Laguna Beach revealed to their friend, May Rose Borum, drama and speech teacher at Tustin High School, and Norman Mennes, an ex-Tustin High drama student who had just returned from military service, that they had long dreamed of establishing a summer stock theater.

Mennes became enthusiastic as they talked and soon he and the Turneys were determined to begin professional summer theater. Their search for a suitable playhouse narrowed down to Orange County, and then someone remembered the well-equipped auditorium at Tustin High School. Within days, the trio was presenting their ideas to a meeting of the Tustin Board of Education. Board members Ben Osterman, Jack L. Bascom, George Veeh, Gene Thomas, Edwin Cox, and Principal Orville Northrup became equally enthusiastic about the project and agreed to their using the auditorium.

The Turneys and Mennes decided on Holiday Stage as the name for their project and spent the winter and spring interviewing people, analyzing Orange County's theater-going habits and determining the types of productions that would be successful. They found that public reaction was varied.

Some people were enthusiastic, others merely lukewarm and some definitely not interested. Fortunately, the response from the *Tustin News*, *Santa Ana Register* and other newspapers was positive, and Holiday Stage became a hot news item.

The first production in a ten-week season that opened in June 1947, was *State of the Union.* Audiences were sparse, and the second production, *Petticoat Fever*, starring Broadway actor Oliver Cliff, was a flop. The third show, *The Royal Family*, also bombed.

Deep in red ink, the Holiday Stage was ready to close when the producers decided to give their project one more chance. Sterling Holloway, starring in *Three Men on a Horse*, was a hit, playing to full houses. Heartened by this success, the producers continued the 1948 and 1949 seasons. But despite its success, Holiday Stage closed, and Tustin was again without theater.

Then in 1952, May Rose Borum began producing theater-in-the-round in the multipurpose room/auditorium at the old Tustin Grammar School on C Street. Ray Agayahan, a Hollywood actor, playwright and director, whom she later married, directed many of the shows. After a few seasons, Cathy and Sherwood Price took over as producers and added children's theater.

It took a while, but Tustin residents eventually became interested in Holiday Stage productions and the idea of Hollywood stars such as John Alvin coming to perform in the community. Despite achieving success, the summer productions ceased after a few seasons. Theater-in-the round and productions for children were tried next, but nothing was very successful until Broadway in the Park made its debut. *Courtesy of Tustin Area Museum.*

Audiences came from all over Southern California for seven successful seasons. Then the Tustin Unified School District took over the C Street auditorium, and the Tustin High School auditorium was torn down.

Several other entrepreneurs ventured into theater-in-the-round, and Elizabeth Howard opened a dinner theater, but Tustin had no summer theater until the Tustin Council for Fine Arts began sponsoring an outdoor production every August in Peppertree Park.

First Dinner House Opens

Back in the '50s and '60s, before chain restaurants made their appearance in Tustin, the community had an abundance of places to eat, all owned and operated by individuals whose specialties ranged from breakfast, lunch and dinner to hamburgers or home baked pie. These were not fancy restaurants but casual cafes where a man was comfortable in his shirt sleeves or working clothes.

Then in 1951, Al Pauck and his wife, Fran, turned a small red bungalow on Laguna Road at the corner of Orange Avenue into a dinner house called the Little Red Inn. This was no casual eatery but a classy restaurant where people dined rather than ate. Men donned coats and ties and women wore their Sunday best.

Interviewing the Paucks after they had been operating the restaurant for four years, a *Tustin News* reporter wrote, "In the charming early American atmosphere of the Little Red Inn you'll dine as an extra special guest, for here everyone receives the warm welcome of Mr. and Mrs. Pauck, owners and managers."

The couple was known for living up to their promise to give all diners a special and warm welcome, in addition to offering a selection of fine foods at exceptionally reasonable prices.

While the owners were probably exaggerating when they described the Little Red Inn as truly one of the show places of Tustin, the small red cottage became a popular place to dine. The Paucks eventually remodeled the original building, adding architectural features such as diamond pane windows and white trim to emphasize the Early American theme. A white picket fence and generous planting added to the charm of the site.

The dining room, with its cozy, comfortable atmosphere, was most inviting. Old-timers in Tustin recall the dinner house favorably, citing sparkling fresh red-and-white-checked gingham tablecloths, cloth napkins, floral centerpieces and soft candlelight. Others remember the gleaming knotty pine–paneled walls accented by comfortable captains' chairs.

The menu served by the Paucks was considered cosmopolitan at the time, offering popular entrees such as fried chicken, fried shrimp and the chef's special steak. Broiled lobster eventually was served in addition to chicken, chops, steaks and seafood, but the restaurant continued to open at 5:00 p.m. on weekdays and Saturdays and 12:00 p.m. on Sunday, closing at 9:00 p.m. Liquor was never served.

In addition to managing the restaurant, the Paucks worked as staff. Mr. Pauck presided over the kitchen as chef, and Mrs. Pauck served as both hostess and server.

The clientele included Hollywood celebrities who came to Tustin for summer theater performances by the Holiday Stage and the Tustin

Hollywood star Merle Oberon, *center*, dined at Tustin's Little Red Inn whenever she was in the area. Chef Al Pauck and his wife, Fran, the owners, claimed that she was their favorite customer. The restaurant, which was successful during the 1950s, closed after Interstate 5 drew traffic away from Tustin. *Courtesy of Tustin Area Museum.*

Playbox. These out-of-towners soon decided that the Little Red Inn was the only place where one could really "dine" in Tustin. With the possibility of seeing Hollywood stars such as Merle Oberon, Jimmy Durante and Barry Fitzgerald, more local diners made reservations. Merle Oberon's description of the Little Red Inn as a "charming place" was considered an excellent recommendation.

The Little Red Inn's popularity continued for years, dwindling only after the opening of the Revere House, Reuben's and Red Hill Tennis Club. Eventually, after Interstate 5 had siphoned traffic away from downtown Tustin and Laguna Road, it served its last dinner.

Newcomers Organize Woman's Club

Prior to 1957, the only social organizations in Tustin for women were the American Legion and Knights of Pythias auxiliaries, church circles and WCTU. But that all changed when Lillian Ruth Beckwith came to town.

She decided that the women of Tustin needed an organization especially for them, something like the woman's club in her former hometown. After convincing nine friends, including *Tustin News* publisher Bill Moses and his wife, Lucille, that it was a good idea, she held an organizational meeting on December 5, 1957, for seventy enthusiastic women.

The first meeting of the Tustin Area Woman's Club (TAWC) was held at the Revere House in January 1958 for 143 charter members. Mrs. Beckwith was elected founding president of the club, which received its official charter from the California Federation of Women's Clubs in February.

The new club held its first fundraiser in March 1958 and raised $210 to benefit the Tustin Youth Center Building. Three special-interest sections formed: American Home (later renamed Home & Garden), Bridge and Mannequins. It was decided to limit membership to two hundred with a waiting list, but as women clamored to join, this regulation was relaxed. By 1960, the club had three hundred members, more than the Revere House could handle, and relocated meetings to the Red Hill Tennis Club. Growth was consistent, and in 1963 the membership reached five hundred. Two years later, it had outgrown the Tennis Club and moved to the Elks Club.

More sections formed to satisfy the interests of the members: Choral, Arts and Crafts, Fine Arts, Antiques, Golf, Book Review, Yearlings, Gadabouts,

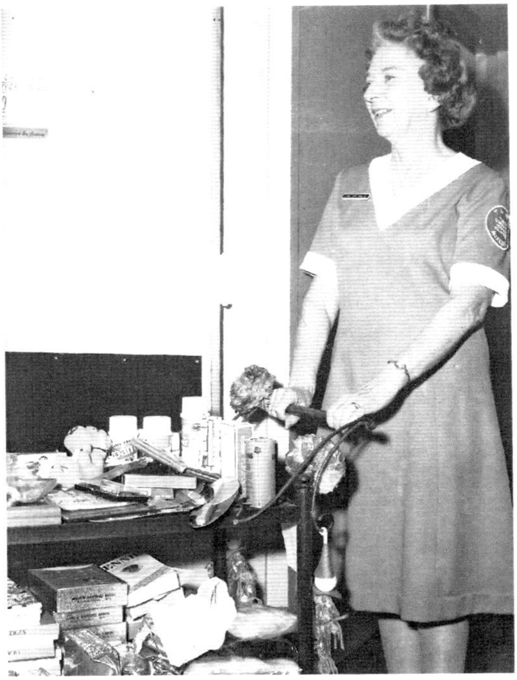

Tustin Area Woman's Club became an active philanthropic and service group after it formed in 1958. Tustin Community Hospital patients always welcomed visits from members of the hospital auxiliary, such as Ida McCalla, who was also third president of TAWC in 1961–1962, with books and other items. *Courtesy of Tustin Area Museum.*

Gourmet, History and Landmarks, Bowling, Canasta and Couples Ballroom Dance.

But these ladies did more than socialize and attend meetings. Fundraising was an important function of the club. Between 1958 and 1967, it donated $35,000 to charities and philanthropic organizations. One of the most unusual fundraisers was the publication of a book written by one of the History and Landmarks section members, Inez Pierson. Proceeds from *Tilda from Tustin* were earmarked for the Tustin Area Museum. In addition, volunteers worked for other organizations such as Services for the Blind, the Albert Sitton Home and Orange County General Hospital.

Tustin's youth also benefited from TWAC. In addition to organizing Tustin Youth Employment to help young people find jobs, the club opened a youth employment office and staffed it. Over the years, it has given hundreds of dollars in scholarships in addition to organizing Artist of the Month and Girl of the Month awards. Girl of the Month began at Tustin High and was expanded as Foothill and Beckman opened. The club has given financial assistance to students at Hillview Continuation School, sponsored youth in the American Field Service Program and adopted Heideman Elementary School in the "Partners in Education Program."

When Tustin Community Hospital opened, TAWC formed a hospital auxiliary to do volunteer work there. In addition to visiting the patients and assisting the staff, the auxiliary operated a gift shop. After the hospital closed in 1996, the auxiliary began to volunteer at Chapman Hospital in Orange.

Tustin Area Woman's Club has provided close to $1 million to hundreds of charities and philanthropic groups since it organized. The women's work has been recognized many times by the California Federation of Women's Clubs, as well as Disneyland, which has given them numerous awards, and the City of Tustin.

Snow Surprises Everyone

Pounding rain followed by a thick blanket of snow covering Santiago Peak and the surrounding mountains, plus temperatures that make one shiver and shake, often have some folks wondering if it ever snows in Tustin.

Old-timers don't speculate—they know the answer. It certainly has snowed in Tustin, twice as a matter of fact. The first snowfall was recorded in the winter of 1881 while Tustin was still a small village. The next time it snowed was in the twentieth century—January 11, 1949, to be exact.

I missed the phenomena because I was away at school, but my mother filled me in on all the details. Since she was born about twenty years too late for the first snow in Tustin, she was in a state of euphoria when she awoke to see snow in the backyard. From her excitement, I anticipated that she would tell me that great drifts of snow covered the roads and orchards.

To my disappointment, she described a storm that had left snow that could barely be measured in inches. White patches covered the driveway, and the shrubbery was frosted like a flocked Christmas tree. The orange trees and the smudge pots were dusted with snow, but all in all, you had to work hard to gather enough of the icy crystals to make a decent snowman.

The sun, which soon penetrated the clouds, melted the white stuff into muddy slush, except in the shade, but not before people grabbed their Kodaks and preserved visions of snow in Tustin for posterity. Family albums contain black and white photos of snow covering lawns and streets, as well as bundled up children scraping together snow for a snowball or a snowman.

Areas on higher ground such as Lemon Heights had more generous coverage than the flat lands of Tustin, five inches in some locales. The *Santa Ana Register* had pages of beautiful pictures showing the miracle of snow throughout the Santa Ana Valley.

Snow fell on Tustin in January 1949 for the first time since 1881, leaving a thick blanket of white on Santiago Peak and the surrounding mountains. Children in town had trouble scraping together enough of the white stuff to make snowmen and a few snowballs, but they were euphoric with the experience. *Courtesy of Tustin Area Museum.*

Old Saddleback, as Santiago Peak is commonly called, rose into the sky at a height of 5,691 feet like a giant marshmallow sundae. The air was crisp and cold, colder than the usual subfreezing weather when smudge pots were lit to protect the trees and puddles and bird baths froze like miniature ice rinks. Agriculture experts claimed that the snow covering the trees protected the Valencias, which would ripen in the spring, and the already ripe navels from freezing.

Years later, if we are surrounded by snow, the mountains are inaccessible or at least two hours away, forcing snow enthusiasts, skiers and snowboarders to put chains in their vehicles and head for the nearby ski resorts. The rest of us enjoy beautiful views of the snow-covered mountains while we are outside and thankfully hover near the fire when we are inside.

First Tiller Day Festivities Organized

It was an early summer day in 1957 when Bill Moses, editor/publisher of the *Tustin News*, and his advertising manager, Clint Caldwell, decided Tustin needed some excitement. Why not organize a parade?

They approached the chamber of commerce with their idea, and soon plans were underway for a parade plus a carnival and a street dance. Then someone came up with the idea of calling the event Tiller Day in honor of the time when Tustin was an agricultural community.

Committees were formed and organizations were approached, and by August the concept of a parade, a carnival and a street dance had become a reality.

People gathered on the sidewalk alongside the First National Bank of Tustin to watch the first Tiller Day parade pass by in 1957. The city's antique firetruck carrying the first Tiller Day Queen and her court, city officials riding in convertibles, horses and few bands were greeted with enthusiasm. *Courtesy of Tustin Area Museum.*

A decent-sized crowd lined D Street (now El Camino Real), considering the designated Saturday morning was hot and there was little shade. Tustin's new firetruck, a shiny red vehicle with gleaming brass, headed the line of march, startling the crowd with periodic blasts of its horn and siren. The city's first firetruck, the converted 1912 Buick donated by Sam Tustin, proudly followed, carrying the first Tiller Day queen and her court. Entries were mainly convertibles carrying Mayor Jerome C. Kidd, city council members, Frank Bacon, Lee Byrd, Vincent L. Humeston, W.L. Tadlock and other dignitaries. Equestrian groups provided variety.

Bands were sparse, but the crowd didn't seem to miss them. They hooted, hollered and applauded as if it was the grandest parade they'd ever seen. The last parade entry passed by, and the spectators moved over to Main Street, which had been blocked off east of D for the carnival. Next to the Tustin Drug Store, musicians used a flatbed truck as their bandstand, playing catchy dance music. Those that performed included Ray Aunger, owner of the Tustin Hardware; Dan Spriggs from Ruby's Cafe; W.R. Nelson, Tustin Elementary School principal and later superintendent of the school district; and Helen and John Gritz, local musicians and piano teachers.

Tiller Day was deemed a success that should be repeated. Someone suggested that more school bands and organizations would be available in the fall, and the date was moved into October. Tustin Area Woman's Club, which had supervised the first queen contest, continued to be involved. The Junior Chamber of Commerce took over the entire event in 1963.

Now a Tustin Tiller Days Committee is in charge of all facets of the project, which has grown to a three-day celebration. Tiller Days has swelled from a few makeshift games to more than one hundred booths, plus a full-scale traveling carnival. Columbus Tustin Park has been the site for many years.

The parade route has changed several times over the years. Units originally marched south from First Street into the heart of the business district, then the route was reversed.

Tiller Days now attracts thousands of people and makes thousands of dollars for Tustin's nonprofit organizations.

Preble Estate Becomes Jamestown Village

The little church in the middle of the Jamestown Village parking lot looks as if it has been part of Tustin for centuries, but it only dates back some fifty-plus years.

The location on D Street (El Camino Real) between Main and Sixth was once an orchard with a magnificent Victorian home owned by George Preble, who came to Tustin in 1876. A builder as well as an orange grower, he built the Tustin Hotel, the Tustin Lemon Association packinghouse and Tustin High School in addition to his home.

In 1955, builder C.T. Gilbreath bought the house, then known as the Franklin P. Crawford house. The property, which had shrunk to about two acres, included a well house and a barn, with two circa 1928 Nash automobiles in it, an orange grove and a few avocado trees.

The Gilbreath family moved into the house and lived there until 1960, when work began on Jamestown Village. The two-story home was offered free to anyone who would move it, but there were no takers, and the house was demolished in October 1960.

The mantel from the old house was given to Walter Knott for use at Knott's Berry Farm. Some of the other interior items were salvaged for use in the shopping center. Gilbreath managed to save many of the pine trees surrounding the house, working them into the landscaping, but he fretted over a large oak tree in the parking lot. Writing in the *Tustin News* in 1968, he explained, "I felt that I should do something special around this oak tree. Flowers? Everybody plants flowers. A tree house? No, kids would get hurt. Then my thoughts drifted back to my childhood in Columbia, TN."

As he reminisced, he recalled 1912 when he had gone with his grandmother by horse and buggy to Hopewell Church. The country church that she had attended from the time of the Civil War was about six miles outside Columbia. Those pleasant memories provided him with the solution for the oak tree.

He designed and built a miniature of his grandmother's church, only with the oak tree growing through the middle of it. The Little Tree Church, with white clapboard siding, a red brick porch and shake roof, still stands but is no longer sheltered by the oak tree. A combination of old age and disease killed it a number of years ago.

Today, the tiny church stands alone in the parking lot with its cupola reaching into the sky. The green trim encasing the stained glass windows

Builder C.T. Gilbreath preserved as many of the trees from the Preble estate as possible when he built Jamestown Village on that property in 1960. A tiny church located at the rear of the shopping center duplicated Hopewell Church, which he attended with his grandmother as a boy in Columbia, Tennessee. The church is often used for weddings. *Courtesy of Tustin Area Museum.*

is fresh, and the interior, with its cathedral ceiling, knotty pine walls and four small pews, appears to be waiting for a wedding or christening party to arrive and light the candles in the sconces. A small white organ stands ready, as does the pulpit made from a large rock elevated on a brick platform.

Gilbreath passed away in 1987, followed by his wife, Charlie May, in 2004. The center is still owned and managed by the Gilbreath family.

NEW BANK OPENS IN FILLING STATION

Only one of all the banks in Tustin can claim to have started life in a filling station and be the first Orange County bank with drive-up teller lanes: Sunwest.

First known as Santiago Commercial Bank, the bank was incorporated in 1968 by a group of local investors. Opening in 1970, the board bypassed fancy digs and took over an out-of-business Mobil Oil service station at the corner of First and D (El Camino Real), offering drive-up banking, a service untried in the county. Lines of pumps were turned into cubicles with windows on two sides and a door at one end. Space wide enough for two cars to pass through at the same time was left between the two little buildings. Each housed a teller station equipped to serve customers who drove up to one of the small windows. Transactions—whether deposits, withdrawals or check cashing—could be completed with the customers in their cars.

The old station building, which dated back to the 1930s, was transformed into a compact bank with a lobby for those who opted to go inside and backroom space for bank functions.

People flocked to Santiago, attracted by the drive-up convenience. After a few years, they outgrew the space and moved operations to a two-story building across from Larwin Square on First Street. Drive-up banking was still offered, with the capacity increased by windows for as many as four tellers on the south side of the building. A double line of cars often snaked along the driveway, awaiting a turn at the drive-up windows.

Tustin's Santiago Commercial Bank, now Sunwest Bank, was unique in that it was the first bank in Orange County to offer drive-up teller windows, as well as the first to open in a out-of-business service station. Incorporated in 1968 by a group of local Tustin investors, the bank now has several locations, all with walk-up or drive-up service. *Courtesy of Sunwest Bank.*

In 1980, the bank reorganized as Sunwest and was acquired by West Coast Bancorp in 1985. Sunwest now has branches in Laguna Hills, Anaheim and Newport Beach. The Tustin branch has been moved to East Seventeenth Street between Yorba and Prospect.

Sunwest was the third home-owned bank to open in Tustin. The first, the Bank of Tustin, organized by members of the Tustin Land and Improvement Company in 1888, occupied a specially built Richarsonian Romanesque building at the corner of Main and D. Overwhelmed by the cost of the grand building, the undercapitalized operation survived the Panic of 1893 but went under in 1902 when the Tustin Hotel defaulted on its loan. The building was used by a drugstore until 1911, when a second bank, the First National Bank of Tustin, was organized and occupied the premises.

This bank operated independently for almost sixty years. Acquired by Lloyds Bank in the early 1960s, it was relocated to a new building at the corner of Third and D, then across town, losing its identity. The old building was torn down shortly after the acquisition.

Now, strangely enough, most drive-up tellers have been replaced by walk-up windows.

Freeway Kills Local Business

Once upon a time there was a small town called Tustin located at the exact spot on the 101 Highway where travelers between Los Angeles and San Diego began to think about filling up the gas tank, stopping for a stretch, a cup of coffee and a snack. Then on October 27, 1955, the newly completed 5 freeway was opened to traffic, and cars began to speed past.

Service stations, garages and cafes that had served the motorists in the past waited, but their only customers were local residents. Some people called this first freeway completed in Orange County a lifeline of Southern California economy, an influence on industrial and residential growth and a taxable value for Orange County; however, for others, it was a sad day when the section circling the west side of Tustin opened.

Basically, the freeway followed the same route as the old Highway 1, except it bypassed the heart of Tustin. With on/off ramps in the early days limited to Tustin Avenue and Red Hill, Old Town Tustin was easily missed.

The $6,550,000 construction project had turned Tustin's central business center into a ghost town.

A *Tustin News* reporter wrote, "Thanks to the freeways for driving time convenience. Tustin area residents couldn't be in a better spot for easy access to major shopping centers and recreations spots." But he forgot that a number of residential streets had been bisected with no way for traffic to pass between the two sections. The many vintage homes, including Los Alisos, where Madame Modjeska had lived while residing in Tustin, and the acres of citrus that had been destroyed meant nothing to him. Nor did he have any sympathy for those with homes that survived the freeway, only to listen to the roar of traffic twenty-four hours a day.

The dozen or so gasoline stations and garages that lined Highway 101 from First and Tustin Avenue to Laguna Road soon felt the pinch of losing the trade of the hundreds of cars that no longer traveled through town each week. Tustin's many cafes and snack shops also suffered. No more thirsty and hungry travelers were dropping in. Even policeman "Big" John Stanton, who had made sure the out-of-town cars observed the speed limits, was bored.

Tustin Garage was the last to close after the opening of the 5 freeway eliminated through traffic in downtown Tustin. Before that, the dozen or so gasoline stations and garages lining Highway 101 from First and Tustin Avenue to Laguna Road kept busy, serving traffic en route south to San Diego or north to Los Angeles, as well as local customers. *Courtesy of Tustin Area Museum.*

Basil F.H. Brewster had foreseen that the freeway would bring fewer overnight customers to Brewster Auto Court and sold his business prior to completion of the 5. As motorists vanished, the new owner decided to turn the cottages into a business complex.

The opening of the 5 coincided with other changes: an influx of new residents, many lured to Tustin by the convenience of freeways; annexation of outlying areas; and the building of tracts of new homes, shopping centers and business plazas. Finally, after the navy closed the lighter-than-air base, Tustin was invited to start a new community on its land. Tustin Legacy and the District are the results.

The City of Tustin has changed a lot in the last fifty-plus years. In 1950, population was 1,143. More recently, it was recorded at 70,350. Fortunately or unfortunately, Old Town has experienced little of this change.

ACTIVITIES CELEBRATE TUSTIN'S CENTENNIAL YEAR

Newcomers to Tustin and even some folks who have been around for a while often wonder why old-timers frequently refer to El Camino Real as D Street. That's because the name was changed in 1968 during the yearlong celebration of Tustin's centennial.

Columbus Tustin and his partner, Nelson O. Stafford, completed the purchase of an undivided one-sixty-fourth of Rancho Santiago de Santa Ana in 1868, although the deed of partition was not signed with Tustin taking possession of almost 840 acres until 1869. Because the plat map was not filed until sometime between August 1870 and May 1871, many historians use 1870 as the date of Tustin's founding; however, the City of Tustin used the year of the purchase for the centennial celebration date.

A.J. "Tony" Coco, who served as mayor from 1968 to 1972, presided over the festivities with the help of a committee of city council members, which, because of the beginning and ending of terms during the year, included five men: Gerald Mack, Ronald I. Klingelhofer, L.E. Marsters, Clifton C. Miller and Duane J. Ring. Harry Gill was city administrator; Ruth Poe, city clerk; and James Rourke, city attorney. The city hall was then located at 135 West Third Street.

A gala dinner dance at the Newporter Inn launched the centennial celebration on February 17, 1968. Most of the movers and shakers in

Tustin attended. Many women, including Mrs. William Leinberger, Mrs. Leon Lauderbach, Mrs. Douglas Gorrie and Mrs. Worth Alexander, wore elaborate gowns from the Victorian era.

President Lyndon Johnson and Governor Ronald Reagan sent messages of congratulation to the citizens of Tustin. Lucille Moses, wife of *Tustin News* publisher Bill Moses, and Lee Wagner, a local businesswoman, planned a number of events during the celebration, including the selection of Centennial Queen Linda Hoffertberg, a home tour and a tea for the ladies. A mayor's luncheon and a street dance were other activities. The *Tustin News* published a special Centennial Report issue featuring the history of the city.

An eight-acre park at Tustin Meadows, a newly built nine-hundred-home walled community in South Tustin, was dedicated to the city and named Centennial Park. Max Tilton of Robert H. Grant Developer, Inc., and

As part of the centennial celebration of the founding of Tustin, Representative James B. Utt, City Clerk Ruth Poe, Councilman L.E. Marsters and Mayor A.J. Coco cut the ribbon at a ceremony renaming D Street El Camino Real. Honored guest Ernest Osuna watched. *Courtesy of Tustin Area Museum.*

representatives of the Irvine Company joined Mayor Coco and the city councilmen at the dedication ceremony.

The centennial celebration climaxed in September with the renaming of D, H, and Fourth Streets. D Street was renamed El Camino Real (the Royal Highway), after the route Father Serra used as he traveled from mission to mission in the prerancho days. Fourth Street, which had retained its Santa Ana name after being extended into Tustin, was renamed Irvine because it joined Irvine Boulevard at Newport Avenue, and H Street became Centennial Way.

The streets received their new names as Representative James B. Utt, City Clerk Ruth Poe, Councilman L.E. Marsters and Mayor Coco presided in a festive dedication ceremony. A parade followed, with Ernest Osuna, a descendent of the Alcaldes of San Diego, as its honored guest. That evening the community continued the celebration at a street dance on Main Street between El Camino Real and Prospect.

Some Tustin officials are already thinking about the city's sesquicentennial in 2018, as well as an incorporation centennial in 2027.

City Annexes Eight Acres of New Homes

Forty years ago, Walnut, Sycamore and Redhill Avenues south of Tustin passed through orange orchards and bean fields. A wall erected around the Irvine Company's bean field at the corner of Walnut and Red Hill was the first sign that a change might be coming.

Soon everyone knew that the Irvine planning staff was working on something. That something resulted in the property being annexed to the City of Tustin and the Robert H. Grant Company being commissioned to build the first Irvine Company–developed community in which the homeowner would own the land under his house and not lease it.

Nine hundred homes would be built surrounding an eight-acre park to be designed by landscape designers Erikson, Peters and Thomas. Called Centennial Park in recognition of Tustin Meadows opening during Tustin's centennial year of 1968, the oval-shaped park would have a central meadow and a myriad of recreational facilities. Dedicated to the City of Tustin, the facility would stress great family fun, with basketball, handball and volleyball courts; swing sets; sand; jungle gyms; and barbecues and picnic facilities.

Once a bean field, Tustin Meadows is now one of Tustin's most attractive residential areas, with lovely curved streets lined with massive trees, beautifully landscaped yards and well-kept homes. Opened in 1968, the development, which is centered by an eight-acre park and has several clubhouses with pools, has been extremely popular. *Courtesy of Tustin Area Museum.*

Six floor plans with fifteen different elevations were planned for the community, which was unusual in that its streets were designed to discourage through traffic. Early prices of $19,995 to $29,995 made the community and its many amenities, including two clubhouses with swimming pools, especially attractive.

Approximately fifteen thousand people visited during Tustin Meadows' grand opening, many taking advantage of horse-drawn surrey tours of the property. Six hundred homes were sold the first year. Many of the new residents became active in the City of Tustin. Don Salterelli and Joe Langley would both serve on the city council and as mayor, Ursula Kennedy became the first woman to be elected to the city council and Jill Leach became *Tustin News* editor.

In June 1968, Tustin mayor Tony Coco presented Tustin's Annual Beautification Award to a Robert H. Grant representative at the annual chamber of commerce dinner. A second trophy was given to the Irvine Company in recognition of its continuing beautification program.

The new development became a close-knit community. A Tiny Tots preschool, baby sitting co-op, Dolphins swim team and Tustin Meadows Woman's Club were organized, contributing to the small-town feeling.

A Fourth of July celebration that began in 1968 continues today as an annual parade.

There were no shopping centers, traffic signals or schools in the area when construction started, but St. Cecilia's Church, Thorman Intermediate and Currie Middle Schools and medical facilities, as well as many shopping centers with fast food, restaurants, groceries, gas stations and other facilities, soon opened.

Tustin Meadows, with massive trees, beautifully landscaped yards, well-kept homes and community spirit, is one of Tustin's most attractive residential areas.

About the Author

As a third-generation resident of Tustin, with her grandparents settling there in 1885, Juanita Lovret has long been interested in the history of the area. After graduating from the University of Southern California, she pursued a career that combined writing, editing and teaching, with local history as her avocation.

She is a longtime member of the Tustin Area Historical Society and has served on the board as publicity chairman and president. In addition, she is a docent at the Tustin Area Museum and has assisted with school tours and the annual home tour. She's written a column based on Tustin history, "Remember When," for the *Tustin News* since 1997.

She was named Tustin Woman of the Year in 1996, received the Tustin Preservation Conservancy's the Spirit of Old Town Award in 2009 and the Elks Distinguished Citizenship Award in 2010.

She and her husband, Clint, have three children, all of whom attended Tustin schools and came back there to live after college. Their six grandchildren are the fourth generation to attend Tustin schools.

In addition to her work as a freelancer, she published a book in conjunction with the Tustin Area Historical Society in 2003. Entitled *Remember When*, it is the story of her childhood on a Tustin orange ranch.